© 2020, Massinissa, Yohan
Edition : Books on Demand,
12/14 rond-Point des Champs-Elysées, 75008 Paris
Impression : BoD - Books on Demand, Norderstedt, Allemagne
ISBN : 9782322209873
Dépôt légal : avril 2020

Educational passions
by Yohan Massinissa

Copyright, 2020, *Yohan Massinissa*

Si vous vous mettez à la place de l'autre, et l'autre où est ce qu'il se mettra ?

Philippe Meirieu.

Educational passions

Yohan Massinissa, Avril 2020.

The staff room is almost empty. At the counter, to my left, further on, William the computer scientist works on his keyboard computer. Two other colleagues, vaguely remembered, may be supervisors around a table, chatting. I take a coffee. It is Thursday. Marie Cecile gets in, looking undecided, and comes to me.
- Yohan, hello. Were-you on the 6th Tripoli council?
-      Yes,
- What has been said about Janna?
- They started by saying "good job", and Saïna added, "Not focused enough. She talks with her neighbor". I didn't say anything. I was listening.
- She plays favoritism for Caetano, who is however disruptive. In sports he doesn't stop fooling around. And Clementine! She knows her mother. Everything is great with her.
- It's true that I often find them, Clementine with Saïna in the parking several times, chatting.

Marie speaks, already almost in tears. Aurelia comes in furtively, walks over to her, puts a kiss on her cheek, and leaves.
She resumes, almost without interrupting.

- I should have Janna in my class. And Odeline did not hesitate to put a remark in Florine's notebook. Would you put a remark in my daughter's notebook?
- No. If I have some things to say, first I would talk to her. I happened to do it. And then if I need to, I'll talk to you about her, like I would for Anthony or Sabia's daughter.

- I should never have put my daughters in this school.
- I notice some clan spirit of good teachers close to the chief. She keeps on drowning us with her multiple intelligences project. And the others colleagues are in total admiration.
- Absolutely.

This afternoon of Monday November 4, I am calm with the three classes. The best moments are obviously with the 5th Prague, whose, Lyna, her sister, Florine and her lovebird Gwendoline and Sicilia. Sicilia is very active and generous. She does her job well and tidies up all the computers.

In the class room of the colleague, Obryan does not deign to look me in the eyes by shaking my hand. He may have the answer in return.

Wednesday November 6, 2019.

I arrive early enough to get my folders and computer out, but not to open the files and turn on the projection.
The work takes place during the 4th Rome and 5th Pretoria sessions without projection. It's better, because, it is ultimately not essential most of the time.

With the 5th, the tone is pleasant, even when there is a need to crop. As for Venissia who talks and tells all the time, I launch "Venissia, your story is fascinating".

While with the 4th Rome class, there is a word in the notebook for Kahina. It's necessary for absence from work during the whole session. She goes without saying the usual "goodbye". With Naomi, a real rant to explain that they do not have to invent another scale, and they must comply with my recommendations as instructions. I told her that she didn't have to copy what she had already done, but that she should continue with the rest of the questions. It's a habit that annoys me very often.

I insist at the end of the session that Naomi brings the material to put them away, in order to normalize the link. She has no hard feelings yet.

Passing by to pick up the 4th grade at 8 am, I come across the blonde girl who waits for her turn at school life. Outside, Clarisse greets me smiling. I see the beers potiche at noon, far outside, without exchange of glance.

I am in the technology room. I show Charline, Victoire and Gwenaëlle the drawings. They love very much. Claudia and Lally greet me from the corridor.

Yesterday, Tuesday, was the gardening session. I make a remark to Ambrine the twin,

- With such a gesture you could lose the "praise". Astonished, she looks and says nothing. It's Florine who answers.
- "She did nothing wrong." I look at her and say nothing. She comes and goes on.
- "I was the one who started".

- "Florine, you know what you mean to me". "I prefer to tell you that for a small gesture, a student loses "praise". Look at Sicilia, Lyna, nobody notices them".

She doesn't seem to like the example of Sicilia.

Towards the end, I call Lyna to show her a drawing, Florine wants to see too, but she understands that she is not authorized. The real problem is that the day before, she accompanied her sister Janna, in the teachers' room. They pass behind the bar, surprising me, when I just wanted to ask the little sister a quick question about her neighbors to redo the groups. Her mom comes in and sees them. She doesn't seem very happy. I am also embarrassed not to have had the time to prevent them from going behind the bar. I quickly made my way back to the 2nd floor to continue the advice of the 5th.

Avoid accumulating questionable incidents. I am not reassured to show a drawing which seems to represent her among others.

It is time to provoke the desire to see these drawings. It is therefore necessary to move on to painting, before proposing new portraits in pencil.

I am in my classroom at a break time. Madison moves into the room to ask a delicate question, and disappears, without goodbye. Never says hello since. I have also ignored her group whenever possible. These students are not reliable.

Florine is a conscientious girl. From the next session, Friday, we will have to take stock with her on the "Praise" objective for the end of the second semester. And it will be an opportunity to know if the drawings inspired by the classroom activities are not a problem.

Thursday November 7, 2019.

The first session with 5th Vienna, a group, we resume the activity of cutting leaflets to illustrate energy conversion. It's very calm, sad limit. Towards the end, some jokes are possible. As I hand an image to Marie-rose, and I add to her "May the light be with you". The atmosphere is defrosted.

They tidy up without insisting too much at the end, all courteous, "goodbye sir".

The next is the 4th Lisbon class. They arrive almost happy, joyful. They enter the new room. They search for their respective places according to the plan. This anarchy breaks the protocol of silence before sitting down.
"Nobody listens," laughs Victorine. They will all listen, replied I. it's less than a minute later, everyone is listening. Thanks to what? Nothing, silence causes silence.
I make a positive remark for Liam. He behaved like a charm during the whole session. To refuse it would be the risk of a break. And I point out to Samuel, "Clara is the one who deserves the most to have a positive remark."
I'm going to see Elisa at 11 a.m. I explain that Damien offers me gardening help with the students by giving me the calendar and ordering the seeds, using his account at Game vert. We exchange, Elisa and me, in the presence of Saïna and Leïlia. She complains about the interference of Obryan F and Jean Marc C, as well as Madame D, in this activity.
I remind you that the technology room, they did not have the concern to grant it to do this work and come as conscientious

managers who want to lead. She complains about Obryan's bad intentions.

Madame D told him "I had the idea", Elisa replied "I have been proposing this idea to you for 5 years".

In the technology room, boxes are being stored. It's a new arrival. The computer scientist explains the concern for cables. I still prefer to ask him rather than to Obryan.

Monday morning Madame sends me Damien to explain the reasons for the delay. According to Jean Marc, it is today Thursday November 07, 2019 that they are supposed to bring back the HDMI cables and the missing computers.

Only the boys salute from the hallway at the storeroom. I don't see anyone but I can hear everyone.

Friday November 8, 2019

I have two more pleasant sessions with the 6th Oslo and Brussels class. It's quite simply calm. The explanation is orderly and reminders to order without too much noise for a few lost.

With the 4th Rome, there is sometimes severe cropping. I make pats on their laziness to remember the instructions and repetitive feints for not having understood the sentence instruction. Simple things like "put away this document now and take this one". They may have come to understand.

Naomi makes me promise to put a positive remark on her if she is wise. She hands me her notebook at the end of the session. I point out to her that often Adriana was listening to her chatting but that there is the best. I then bring up the case of a student to whom I have done this favor. She answers "Liam?" I ask "how do you know this", Malya admits that "they have been in love for eight months".
- "He's a good boy", I answer.
- "You are jealous?" Naomi asks me.
- "No, it's the opposite. It's when you're with fools that I'm jealous. But you chose the best".
- "Naomi, can you bring the equipment back?"

She arrives with the fan radiator.

- "Why are you always asking me help?" she smiles as she understands. No need for me to explain.

November 12, 2019

The afternoon of Friday November 8 is spent with the Prague. I demand almost complete silence to end the brochure clipping activity. Sicilia finishes very quickly. I put her on the machine to do an activity that she had not had the opportunity to do in sixth grade. Janelle joined her a few minutes later. Towards the end of the session, I signal to Florine to come and "see what I had shown Lyna on Tuesday, so that you are not upset." I then show her the drawings.
- What do you think of this machine?
- Ah yes, this is the machine from last year? It is well done.
- Thank you.

I then invite her to return to her place. The answer is not surprising given her hesitant and questioning gestures when I ask her to come and see. A sign of the hands and the eyes rather towards her comrades "that is what he wants me" "why he gives me importance" and her attitude of these last days with the neighborhood far from being wise.

The challenge is to take up the objective of obtaining "Praise" at the end of the semester.

I notice that at the exit, the students were a little amused.

With the 5th Pretoria class, the session is more pleasant. It's funnier they understand and take better the remarks on the behavior.

At the 3:20 p.m. break, Charline, Victoire and Galiane came in with relief that they hadn't come for nothing, seeing me.

I tell them first the anecdote about the total indifference of a person for these drawings of a pupil of 5th Prague. Charline guesses that "it's Florine".

I hope they approach her to explain her reaction or her lack of reaction.

These three girls look at the drawings and chat. I let them watch everything. I have no more reliable in the establishment. I listen to them speak and comment on the drawings. I can listen to them for hours because they know how to talk about. They notice things. Lines, colors, resemblances that make them think of people. It is necessary to find a time slot to replace this passage at 3 p.m. I then think of involving them in my journal writing.

Two drawings catch their attention. "I think I've met her before, it reminds me of someone".

It is 12:10 p.m., Madame D has just left Ingrid, who has been inspected. She walks into my room to point out the change of a few tables that she had made to get more harmony in the rows. When she knew computers were long overdue and late, we've been working without it for 9 days. She does not say a word on the subject. The others haven't told me yet. The other room is already equipped. I may not be responsible enough for her to tell me about it directly.

I'm learning a lesson there. It's that I must always point out what I've done, otherwise nobody pays attention.

This morning, with the sixth, a new method is tested. It's about shortening the sequences, more effectively. The students are very pleasant. With the 6 Topazes, the link is very cordial, including Fantine, Calypso... and Olivia. They are warmer.

At the 11:15 a.m. break, Clarisse passes by, but doesn't even take a look.

During the 10:20 break, Julie and Adenise, pass in the corridor and turn around with a beautiful smile and a wave. I answer with a silent hand sign. I dare not show them the drawing, it is not finished.

Elene walks by the door, stops and greets me out loud. I say hello "Elene".
I think for a moment about showing her the drawing of a person close to her. There is not enough time.
I send a message before 7 am to Dany B. He is technology teacher in Victor Hugo School in the region. I ask to participate in Cartec Technology training and creation. I've been trying to reach him for several weeks. He received my message in his locker according to the secretary I just got on the phone. He never deigned to answer. I feel contempt in the air. It is time to move on. I think to the creation of a Cartec between private and public school, with Jean Daniel for example.

Wednesday November 13, 2019

In the teachers' room, Marie Dax comes in. We greet each other from a distance, but warmly.
- "Sicilia, What does she have? I saw her on a crutch in the hallway".
- "She had an accident, fallen on the grid". She then explains the accident.
Elisa gets in the room. Tell me about the achievements of the 5th Prague gardening. They made a hedgehog shelter. "I'm waiting for Sicilia to present it to the students," she replies. There is no reason to justify this patience. But it's nice to please people you want to please. Marie Dax, Sicilia mom, does not say a word on the subject.
We exchange, Elisa and me, on the follow-up to the current activities. She is interesting. But each time in her answers she wants everyone to hear and be passionate about it. She has always difficulty to make the distinction between simple idle conversations and professional exchange. She wants to tell all the proposals and each of the students' sketches, like she usually does. And as usual, I bring her back to the

main objective. Like the work to prepare for the next session more concretely.

Madame D comes in to get some coffee. I let Madiba make one for her. To whom she just kissed. Not for me. But she pulled herself together and said hello to me. But the hugs between both of us are tacitly suppressed reciprocally.

Elene, Sarah and Léon pass by the door at 10:05 am and greet me. I answer and ask to wait a moment. I show a drawing.

- It's you? Elene asks. Understand "you did it?"

- Yes,
- Ah, it's Lana...! Lana, I haven't seen her since the exchange we had on Cross Day. She was that day accompanied by Clarisse.
- "It looks nice"! Says she, or something like that.
- Goodbye, they're leaving.
- Goodbye.

The session with group 5th Pretoria is going very well. They have a written work to do independently. But the exchange, answers to questions are possible. Sometimes calm reminders are necessary. But the scattered compliments and other pleasant gestures were not for nothing.

Leon and Clara are the best as usual. The nicest... the most beautiful too, and it's not their fault.

It is 11:15 am, I leave, and the 5 Moscou get in the class room with the colleague. Arranged, Adeline at the head, when I leave I say hello to everyone. She says hello, and I just ignore her. Just like throughout the session, since I come back to help finish the installation of the computers that I had started during my session. The reason is her distance from her former friends, Charline, Victoire and Galiane. I have bad memories of the last session with her too. I ask her for help on my computer. She begins, then, she left her place to a certain Roxane, with whom I have no connection. So that I make her model and 3D print a model with her first name. I did it so as not to offend her friend Florine. But I decided to stop giving gifts.

Thursday November 14, 2019

This morning, I start with the session with the group of 5th Vienne. Lisa is absent. She is the charm of this class. But the atmosphere is rather pleasant, with no joke possible. It's a little cold. I do Frequents updates on the attention and application of the instructions. Kalid, is Ilhem's brother.

Ilhem is now in the last year of the high school. I hand him a cut of washing machine, he ignores it. I'm explaining to Nasrine, the others don't listen. Gaspard leaves and refuses to pick up the catalogs. He is far from his exemplary big sister Faouza, the same age than Ilhem. Just like Kalid who does not evoke anything Ilhem. Nasrine on the other hand reminds me terribly of Laelle.

With the 4th Lisbon class, the session is very relaxed. They follow, they work. But cropping interferes with threats of punishment for some who chatter during the explanation.

Between Victorine and Liam, a flame may take.
At the end of the session, I quietly signal Victorine to come. I give her the folder of drawings. She evokes a single first name "Juliette", and continues to look.
At the end, I ask her
- "Did you say Juliette?"
- Yes
- "Juliette who?"
- "Juliette C" she replies, and shows me the photo made in pencil, almost forgotten.

I do not react. I do not say anything. Others also watch, the three boys, Edgar, Aylan and Samuel ask to see. I pass them the folder. "They are well done," they comment.
Victorine recognizes Julie. The boys recognize her too.
I go down at the end of the session to the teachers' room. Elisa announces that she had found planks. They are in the premises of the establishment. I can't get the answer to the question "when will we go get them". Because when she speaks, she explains. Every time I have to stop her. She continues on her father's purchases. She is an old French girl from the hinterland. You have to

get patience. She is always courteous. Attention and tact are her strong points. She has so much knowledge of the campaign too.

Coming back into the building again, I see Adeline entering the hall from the corridor. She looks at me then ignores me, and steps back. As if she was retracting. I leave the hall to enter the corridor. I meet her almost shy smile on my left, and she says "hello sir". I answer "Juliette". "I say Juliette, Adeline, sorry". She smiles, the slip-up amuses her. The slip-up is a simple consequence of that she terribly evokes Juliette at her age.

Three years ago, I asked Juliette to come over to the office to manipulate the mouse. I was demanding. Reality, I seemed very severe. I was myself annoyed because of a comrade who wanted to accompany her but only disrupted the instructions.

Juliette was dressed in a light brown coat this morning. Get a red hood and a blue jean. White sneakers, Nike I think. I did not see her in profile when I got my things from the car. I could recognize her just by her looks. Feet timidly posed, almost with hesitation on the ground with little determination. I haven't seen her smiling since the middle of last year.

I'm going to see Odeline at 11:00 a.m. I meet her in the hallway. She informs me that the appointment for the return of William is in 15 days. A Wednesday, she begins to explain the delay to me. I explain it to her more technically. She is amazed and astonished, grimacing with an abused air of this delay. One day instead of 2 hours.

I explain that he disassembles each computer to install the SSD hard drive to copy the software. However, I had just replied to a student, Ethan, sent by the colleague, that it is next Wednesday that the computers will be usable.

It is 3:20 p.m. Julie and Adenise with Alia find me on the reserve.

- I was told you drew me.
- I signal not to go too far into the room of the reserve by going out with them to repel them, to receive them without offending them.

I step back to take the folder. I give it to them so they can see.

They name recognizable faces.
- She's Janna's sister.
- This one is Juliette.

They fall on that of "Julie". She seems to appreciate and asks
- I can make a copy.
- I promise to make it as soon as it is finished. Marie-Ann's sketch is not finished. I don't know if she recognizes herself.

Friday November 15, 2019

Around 1:20 pm, I meet 5th class in the hall, only Adeline turns to me with a beautiful smile. I then respond with the famous "Adeline" extended. She is not dissatisfied with it.
This morning Naomi asks when entering class,
- "Is it true that you draw people?"
- I promise to answer you at the end of the session.

The session is going very well. They look at the drawings. They identify similarities.
- She and she is Juliette. This one is Jeanne's sister. S, it is very similar.

- "Can we have a drawing of us"? Ask Malya and Naomi.

- "I can't make any promise". But I take pictures of Alia, Malya and Naomi.

I intend to sketch that of Naomi. Alia if I have time it will come. The other I don't think. She and her cousin are not clear. Last year she never said hello.

For the first time, it is 3:20 pm and the three old 6th Brussels do not come. I see them at 3.35pm from afar. A look from Victoire explains me something, by her gaze as she said hello at mid day.

In the hall, Lana and Clarisse don't turn to say hello, nor did they at 4.30 p.m. when leaving the establishment.
But yesterday Thursday at 3.35 pm when they were entering room 115, a furtive greeting from Clarisse and Lana were frank.
In 5th Prague, at Gwendoline's table, the only reason they raised their hands is to go to the toilet. Unlike the girls, their neighbors Paolo and Rayan participated. Sicilia has a flawless session, as usual.

Monday, November 18, 2019
It is 3:20 p.m., break time, I'm alone. I look, I see Fernandine. Not alone, she leaves, she returns. She shows up at the door, followed by Coline and Juliette.
- "I was told you drew me", asked Juliette.

- "She is honored", adds Fernandine.
I hadn't seen that smile from Juliette in over a year.
- "I don't commit to anything. I tried".
- "Why did you draw Juliette?", "Is she your favorite?" "She is very beautiful? She's really beautiful". Supports Fernandine.
- "I don't have to say otherwise".
There they do not seem to understand the double negation.
- "It's because Juliette hasn't smiled in a year". I answer.

Juliette doesn't stop laughing, but quietly. She is turned to Fernandine, as if to hide it. I hold out the binder.
- "I'll let you see".
They turn the pages. They identify faces, similarities. Fernandine recognizes Juliette, the first portrait, then the 2nd

- "Very similar" says Fernandine.

They especially recognize the 2nd. Juliette asks at least three times
- "Where did you find the photo?"
I don't answer. Juliette recognizes "Tiago Michel' friend, Julie or Janelle, and Lana. The others recognize Julie.

- You drew her more beautiful than in real life, says Fernandine about Julie. She is also recognizing Louise Marie.
-       I do not like her. Juliette adds. I admit that I have a vague memory of when she says "I don't like her", is this for Louise Marie, Julie or Janelle. In none of the three cases would I like her declaration.
- They chat for a while, without me. I rarely feed a few words. Tired and I enjoy listening to them.
- How is it going in 3rd grade, in technology?
- "I think we should go". Answer Juliette while looking at Fernandine with a smile. I have the right of interpretation.

They leave, all three say "goodbye". I don't remember a word from Juliette about the quality of the drawings. Rather, it seemed to call into question the two drawings supposed to evoke her modestly.

It remains, to cash later, to get a recent photo of her. In exchange I give her the photo at the base of the drawings. It's In order to be able to do a real portrait painting. But before this bargaining, some

paintings will be needed which will embellish room 112.
Obryan agrees to go to Room 115 every Monday at 11:15 a.m. and free up the classroom 112.

The colleague is very proud to have turned on the video projector in 115, when I showed no sign of it when she had the same concern in 112, before I solved the problem. Another lesson in knowing how to value One's exploits.

Tuesday November 19, 2019.
From 8 am I meet Anthony. He is less warm than usual. I've noticed that last night.

I'm doing a session with the Tokyo, the class of Fantine Dustin. It's Efficient and pleasant. Then I have the 6th Kiev. I spend a lot of time helping them, in particular Clementine. She seems sad. She's alone, nobody hears her when she's talking to everyone out loud.

I spend more than two hours picking up the equipment to do the personalized support sessions with the 5th Prague. When I leave the room, I have to take care of the equipment and storage, while it is the colleague's meeting. I make the students work and I do not agree with her tendency to do everything and let the students observe, by bringing small touches, a screw, a tool. I opt for student involvement. I introduce Florine to drilling with an electric drill. Elisa disagreed. I force her hand courteously. This is her session, but I help for the students and not without the students.

The first hour alone with the 5th Prague, begins more and more cold. First, Elisa and Lyna want to take time off to go to the library.

There is noises and Lack of focus. I threaten to punish. It's Almost a refusal to get involved. It's going bad atmosphere. Iris creates an overly relaxed atmosphere. I'm threatening to kick her out of the team. So her friends are at the height of their discontent, especially Florine and Gwendoline. I run "you begin to be hateful" especially to Florine and Gwendoline. I hardly answer their question.
Sicilia asks, when will we be drilling and screwing with the machines. I point out to

her that her neighbors don't even dare to draw a line on a sign. "The work will not be done by itself".

I ask Florine to do the tracing. She refuses to do so, without saying "no". She remains static in her chair. I understand that you have to type elsewhere. I ask her "Florine you give me back your work!" », Take out your technology folder. I show her the duty that had to be done. I explain calmly.
- I will put flyers in your copy, you can finish at home.
- Okay

I give her the opportunity to finish it in class, as long as she gets ahead. This is where the tension starts to drop and becomes friendlier about the end. At the end of the session, Florine and Gwendoline leave with a "goodbye" a beautiful smile that I have not seen these last sessions since the drawing.

Elisa unblocks the situation for me, because she suggests adapting the available wooden panels directly, without cutting them out. It thus solves the difficulty of teamwork.

Elisa does not follow my advice when I suggest that she drill a diameter of 3.5 for the screws in D4 mm. I then do it my way with Florine and Lyna. While she works with Sicilia and Janelle at hers. She cannot use the available screws, forcing Damien to go and find others.
The difficulty that she could have is the distribution of the activity on several groups while ensuring the autonomy of the pupils. But her spirit with children is more conciliatory and often more educational. The technical method, on the other hand, does not leave enough space for the involvement of the student who remains too spectator and limits admirers.

Adenise and Julie visit me and I take advantage of showing them the almost finished drawing. I give Julie a photocopy of "hers".
- Thank you. A beautiful smile from the two precedes a very warm "goodbye".

At 4:00 p.m., I go out into the courtyard to take pictures of the college. Bad luck, the 5th Prague has sport. I still take photos, without the students. Christian comes to me and warns me that the students seem suspicious of my intentions "he takes a picture of us, he draws us". I reassure him that I do not take photos of them. I reaffirm it a moment later to the students themselves in some annoyed and insistent tone. They are both surprised, trying to reassure.

It is certain now that I will no longer draw these 5th grade pupils.
I may try to draw Leon, to please Nathalie. I should especially not try the Venissia portrait, even less Sicilia one. I will try no one in this class.

If I paint the school, it is not to please anyone, especially not adults, but to challenge and prove something to me. That's all. I have to paint recognized places and characters where they are looked at.

Friday November 22, 2019.
I hung up a painting last night. I have done it the same evening, during parent-teacher meeting hours. No appointment. But three

parents came to see me out of the blue to reassure them.
No student noticed the paintings except Roxane.
- Did you draw the picture? She asked me the day after.
- Yes.
- They are very well.
- Thank you
She had participated well during the session. She reminds me that she hadn't had a positive remark during the 5th. I ask her for the notebook. I notify a positive remark. She is very happy with that. She smiled at me several times during the evening.

So I think at the end of the day, as no one else has said a word about the paintings, that if a dead cat was hanging from the ceiling, they wouldn't have noticed.

The next part begins with the 5th Prague. Curiously many do not say hello. The twin, Florine, Gwendoline, Iris, some boys, Ambrine the bad one, all of them, none say hello. The latter was in tears during the session. I don't feel like asking the cause. I nevertheless let her go out for a moment. I signal to Maria to accompany her.

The session is apparently not stormy. Tiago hands me by the beginning his notebook. His mother accuses me of having grabbed his son's arm too strongly. I admit it. I explain that it was to avoid a dangerous gesture. I promise him on the spot never to put a tool in the boy's hands again. And I close with an apology without too much conviction. I notice the students' surprise at the speed of the response written in the notebook. They look at each other.

Students answer more than once, at each step, that we have already done. When I ask, they don't have the right answers. If they don't feel ridiculous, then there is reason to worry.

A chat begins. I begin to bear it less and less. And I react very calmly.

- I'm going to pick up two or three notebooks. And you will understand. You are chatting, and then it will be something else.

I immediately think of this 5th that I had at Saint Jean Barthélemys School in 2013. That time I lost the ability to speak calmly very quickly without it being visible that I was stressed. The voice changes and breathing is disturbed. Today is different. I keep calm until the end. I go up in the gradation of the tone with admirable calm.

- I'm very angry, so be very careful.
Bad words come to mind. I hold myself back. I continue the session, I question. Students participate. Florine raises her hand once to give two good answers on solar energy. I notice that seem enough to make her joyful.

By collecting the homework, I ask nothing of Florine. I see that she doesn't hold anything out for me. I don't watch her. She explains me that she had not had time. I answer her
- "You can bring it back as soon as you have finished it".

Besides, she also does not give me back the work that I had already done to her friends for two weeks. However, I had made the task easier by putting clippings of flyers in her copy to finish it at home. I have no intention of asking her for it again. It is quite possible that I do not put appreciation in the first semester bulletin.

The session ends with more goodbye than hello. Florine said goodbye to me, but I barely hear her, I was talking to someone. So I don't answer.
The 5th Pretoria arrives. They are nicer than the previous ones.

Yesterday's other resolution was to take no photos of students throughout the year. I will take no one, absolutely no one. Not even faceless activities alone. Because often when we start with simple photos of the models made, and it ends with group photos. At 6 p.m. begins the evening of awarding of certificates to former students.

Some students are coming to see me. First Naomi, my 4th grade student approaches, talks, we exchange some word and she asks if we could take a photo. I say yes. She is about to take a self portrait. I say, no, we're going to take a photo. She then asks

"Madame?" Ingrid takes does It. Naomi gets photo with her and two of her comrades. Lina shakes my hand. Naomi was with Fernandine for a while. I ask her to signal the other to turn around.

- Fernandine, I want to talk to you.
-         Yes. Smile.
- "The girl who came with you, I think she didn't like the drawings".
- Who, Juliette?
- Yes.
- "She found it very well done. She is honored" answers Fernandine.
- "Ah yes, what is it well designed Juliette", Add Naomi.
- I am then reassured.

I take the opportunity to explain to Fernandine the context of the photo, suggesting that she tells Juliette.
Fantine, Calvyn's sister sees me, looks at me, doesn't even smile. Boys pass by and greet me. A boy I see in the boxing gym, even face to face, walks past me, and completely ignores me. Whereas in the boxing gym it's the always opposite. I pretend not to know him by having him in front of me. The

second time, he says "Mister" to me. And we punch ourselves right after that. He keeps a pleasant mood even if the levels are far from being comparable.

Laura, an ancient 5th Sarajevo, greets me and kisses me. Lina S, shake my hand. Others wave to me, smiling, like Saïna and Kimberly.

I spend most of the evening with Samuel and Victor's dad, my old and my current student. He promises to show me behind the scenes of the July 14 fireworks. He reminds me of his promise to fly light with Samuel when he turns 20 hours.

We take a drink, at his invitation. Gabriel and Fleure's mom joins us. We redo the presentations. We fix knowledge. She confirms that Gabriel and Fleure were happy to have me. Except that in the evening a certain Maxence just kissed. And Gabriel looks at me in passing and gives me no sign. Fleure comes to see her mother. See me but don't look at me. She was my favorite of the 5th and the 6t. She takes care to stand behind her mom to avoid me by talking to her.

Sabia passes, we exchange a few words. She is radiant. I tell her that I am angry. She suggests that I erase the school after going out in the evening. She is looking for Aurelia. She doesn't seem to find her. On leaving, she passes very close, we exchange two words. Smiling, she leaves.

Christele's mom suggests that she come to greet me. It is a kiss. Well done. Thank you.

Amelia, Lynda and another ancient Sarajevo, come to greet me, very warmly. We chat for a while before leaving.

Former regular visitors, none came. Their names should not be mentioned. But the lesson is that this year, students will want to get a gift at the end of the year and they won't get it. I could make an exception, for some ones, like Fantine D, perhaps Victor and Roxane B.

Abigaelle, Roxane's older sister, although looking much younger, after receiving the patent, approaches me. I hope for a second that it is to greet me. Not even a "hello" formality.

- Sir, don't you know where the trash is?
- "No idea" Did I answer, after a moment of hesitation. She leaves.

I notice the absence of Christine and her son Anthony. He was one of those visitors. My interest in Anthony is only the respect I have for his mom. Just like Charlène, Viviane's daughter. And it's starting to be the case for Florine. While this is not the case for Sicilia, for whom I may have more consideration than for her mother who is quite kind and very kind to friends. She is a daughter of venerable respect and seriousness.

I greet Victor's dad and Fleure's mom, and I leave the room.

Monday 25 November 2019

The morning went without a hitch, with Sixths and fourths.

By the start in the afternoon, everything is going well with the 5 Tirana and the 5 Vienna. But the anxiety is there. When the last hour arrives, I feel that with the 5 Prague, it will be the most intense hour of the day. They come back to class one by one. They say hello shyly.

I explain the purpose of the session, in palpable stress. I end up putting the models on the table. It's supposed to be one of the most educational highlights of the year. I do not tell anyone but I do nearly the program of the 4th.

They still find an enthusiasm to touch and see the model. A craze that dissipates for some, rather some, Florine, Edwige, Iris and even Janelle in front of the documents they have to complete. "I do not understand anything ". This is the leitmotif sentence of these four girls. While the others, Paolo, Rayan and Léon respond and discuss, and show a real scientific curiosity in the investigation.

Elisa, if you don't want to or can't answer, then, you don't have to. At the end, she has rather a good note.

Florine does not approach the document. She repeats "I don't have the answers".
There are ten minutes left, so I ask Florine to isolate herself to finish her homework that all her friends had done a week earlier. I pick them up. I promise to return the work to him to finish it or revise it if necessary. She responds shyly, shaking her head. The session ends cold. Goodbye anyway audible. She has for this work 5/20 and a 13/20.

Tuesday November 26, 2019

I carry Florine's work into the courtyard. She was with Gwendoline, I give them to her. They are more playful. I don't expect to see the shock at the sight of the notes.

Thursday November 28, 2019

It's the ten hour break. The students are gone. I'm at the computer. Marie Cecile arrives in the room. She greets me from the door.

- Hello Yohan
- Hello Marie Cecile.
- Yohan, I'm upset. You put a 5 to Florine. Are you going to put that in the transcript?
- Not impossible. I told her to do the work again. I would never do that for Florine.

- She said to me "he didn't let me finish a homework, and to finish another job".

- Yes, they were blocking on an activity. I'm not hiding from you that right now it's difficult with the 5th Prague.
- I know. They say you draw them. You take a picture of them. Even you drew me …their parents can turn against you.

- I didn't take a picture of them. The drawings are based on photos from a certain era.
- I said "you are catching up on your homework".
- It is a duty for which she was absent ?
- No, she was there. But she hadn't finished it. She was not the only one. Her comrades had returned it the previous Friday.
- She also tells me that you were removing her permanence.
- "It was always to make up for a homework, but I don't do that anymore, I didn't do it last week because I didn't feel it".
- You would then have to give her homework to do it at home.
- It's homework that she couldn't do at home.

I then show her the folder. She begins to watch. She does not arrive at the drawings in question. I promise to see her again. I assure her that she will not get those bad grades. She was very courteous. I see watery eyes. It's impossible to be rude to this woman.

In the evening in the staff room, I let Anthony finish singing with his guitar, and question him if he could hear the noises in the hallway. He explains to me what Christian said to him in the photos. I was right.

- "Christian repeated what he was told, but not what I was trying to say to him, since he had not listened to me".

I then express this annoyance to Anthony. I explained my approach from the start, and handed him the binder.

He recognizes Louise Marie, Lyna, I don't hear if he mentioned other names. He is admiring. He recommends that I also draw boys. I recognize that it is a fault that I concede, probably the only one, that of having drawn only girls.

Friday November 29, 2019

At 1:30 p.m. I receive the 5 Prague. By the way, I notice that Zoéline T, who was looking at me in passing, carefully avoided my gaze by projecting hers towards an indefinite horizon, in a totally neglected way, as it always has. It's the way you look for your comrades, or understand a situation further.

And going towards the course, I perceive the presence of Lana. She makes no sign, but I avoid her just as well.

The majority of the 5 Prague say hello, Florine, Gwendoline, the boys. The twin sisters I don't remember.

Florine is rather cheerful. She asks to distribute. She asks questions. She is happy to understand and to do. She's with Edwige on the computer. She does Arduino programming.

Iris comes to apologize at the beginning of the session for forgetting her notebook. She comes another time later to ask if it is possible to repeat her assessment. She has a bad grade.

The general attitude changes a lot compared to the last one. The cause of this effect remains to be known.

When she leaves, Lyna turns around and looks at me but doesn't say goodbye. Ambrine on the other hand says goodbye
I have a rant with the 5th Pretoria class because of the chatter and the ease of the hubbub taken in recent sessions, for

nothing. They did the same thing the last time, laughing at the choice of the two students who were distributing, while Madame passed in the corridor.

I feel they got the message perfectly. I take the time to put everyone on their post, without hurrying, by mastering each stage of the session. I only put a gate model instead of the previous ones. I change the class plan within the session. Venissia starts spinning bad cotton. She may be having a little too much fun with Naomi and the others. I separate them. It's often delicate situation, as often with the children of friends.

In the morning, with the sixths there was a moment of severity and annoyance, facing a boy who answered "yes", "what" to each whenever I called him, distracted. But the whole is very calm, rather pleasant.

With the 4th Rome, there is a very controlled session. An evaluation followed by the start of a new sequence. In reality, everything rests on calm. The reaction to the behavior is controlled. Not too tolerant, no

anger, no exaggeration and non-educational gesture, even less feeling.
The moment with Kahina recalls the scene of Columbo with his superior.
She finds it difficult to enter the assessment. She seems to refuse to repeat, and is looking for excuses.
- "I do not understand". She replies complaining.
- Kahina, you have to stay positive
- You want to pass this evaluation
- Yes, but
- It's good
- You keep hope
- Yes, but I...
- All right, that's what you have to do...
An exchange for a moment, each time I interrupt her before she addresses the negative sentence.
At the end I hear her say....
- "He didn't let me speak" She complains to her friend Roxane, died laughing like many in the class.

Monday December 2, 2019
I enter the teachers' room, for the first time I no longer say the usual "hello ladies". I'm kissing Taiss the friend. I see Marie Cecile

from behind, pulling her things out of the satchel. Then I kiss Marie rose. I ignore Viviane the dark brunette and Madame, who return it to me just as reciprocally. I come out of the other door, on the courtyard side.
With the 6th Tripoli, Janna participates with great joy. Zoéline loves to distribute documents. She talks to me very often. She is a girl like Lana, very mature. Clementine, when you have already known Alezia, you are rather disappointed with her tendency to have too much fun.
The 5th Vienna, without Lisa, is a sad class.

I am with 5th Tirana. It's a class that we do not remember much. Very few had done homework. So we had to finish everything in class. I come back to the concept described by Patrice Meirieu. Students need time to work. And homework's are a burden from which they want to be relieved. You have to accept to move slower with them, doing the essentials.

With the 5th Prague, the students were well applied in computer work. But this time it is the boys who try the provocation throughout the session. Towards the end I take Cléandre and August away from the computers. Just

like stone a little bit. Cléandre apologizes and I answer without concession "for the moment I do not accept your excuses, I will think about it next session, the slightest deviation, a sanction".
His words at the exit, just before the gate, are another proof of his desire to push the limits. It will therefore require a sanction to prepare for the next session, such as the notebook and isolation. At the back of the room he will hide less when he tries to make sound effects to annoy. His comrades, clearly less intelligent, follow and fall into the trap.

Tuesday 03 December 2019
   I receive a message at the reception that Bastien. He wanted to see Viviane and me. He left the phone number. Viviane, to whom I show her photo, no longer remembers him. I only tell him that he was a good boy.

   By showing the photo, I ask Viviane if she remembered the blonde, Lefèvre. She recalls that he was not interesting, but that today he is very cute.
- I met him again in high school. He's very beautiful. Her brothers too, she notes.

With the 6th Tokyo, I do cropping without looking into the eyes of the first concerned. I do it, without raising the tone. It's effective. They finally understand. I realize that only the boys really participate, like Ambroise, Abraham and Tiago. Tiago is my new favorite. It is necessary and sufficient to balance with the girls by him alone. There are always these girls who create the atmosphere, like Fantine, Juliette, Calypso and Tassiana. They sometimes go to the limits. I often do cropping because of them.
With the Kievs, I realize it's a good class. Girls are very willing.

The afternoon is spent with the Prague personalized support gardening. I don't have all the tools I need. I therefore suggest to those who wish to do so the revision. And let those who wish to build. It left me space to start the activity quietly.

A team of boys, Sam and Simon, are pretty serious. They did the right job.
Sicilia and Janelle have traced. The Gwendoline team did the work too, but it was with them that I spent most of the session. Not for fun, but because otherwise

they would spend their time having fun. I maneuvered gently to get them to finish the construction without breaking their enthusiasm. It is above all Iris who sets up this unhealthy atmosphere. Gwendoline and Florine easily fall into the trap.

Florine likes to put her wet tongue on the board to draw things.
- What is Florine doing? What did she eat?
- No, she puts her tongue to draw.
- I'll tell Janna that!
-… "Florine!" She is dead with laughter and… with shame.
The activity is on its way. The boys do the tracing before the piercing.
I ignore my promise on the notebook to keep Tiago away from the tools. I make him participate.
Florine was away. Not involved. I call her. She approaches hesitantly.
- You have the choice, either you revise, or you participate in the construction
- They don't let me participate.
- Girls, let Florine make the following screws with Gwendoline.
And Florine gets better involved.

I ask her a moment later to look at the tracing made by Sicilia, and to measure to make one on the box.
She is applied with a certain enthusiasm. I see Florine a moment later tracing with Sicilia. And they both rectify, alone, the incorrectly centered screw connections.

At the second hour, Elisa gets in. She takes over. I realize right after Elisa does the work almost by herself, and the students who are supposed to help her have fun or chat. The goal is not to get the job done. But it's for the students to do it.

I suddenly notice a phenomenon. Students draw. I'm taking Edwige's notebook. I find a couple, in love drawn there. I ask Sicilia, I show the boy.
-       Who is it?
- It's me, replied Maxence.
-       Oh yes it's true. I see the resemblance of the eyebrows and the eyes.
Camilia calls me out.
- You want to see my drawings sir.

She hands me some A4 sheets. I find pretty girls there. Another one presents boy and animals.
- You do know how to draw sir? Camilia G asks me.
- I can't say that. But I draw. You have paintings in the room.
- Did you make them? Elisa Asks Camilia.
-    Yes
- They are very well done, replies Marie.
-    Thank you
I return the drawings to Camilia.
-    They are magnificent. For your age you already draw like that!
- Smile.
- Are you joining the fine arts? Ask Elisa
- No, answers Camilia.

I pass in the room and I find Giovanni drawing characters. Iris is drawing a pretty girl with dots on her face. Gwendoline also draws. Finally, the twins were also what they did during the session. That meant that they often tore leaves.

The first gardening session started and went well, it continued like this.

Unlike the previous session, I did not stay until the end of the session, but 20 minutes after the bell rang. I didn't even go back to help them with the tidying up.

In the evening, I receive parents of students. The most significant is Liam's mom. She came without appointment.

- I'm just going to say hello. I'm Liam's mom.
- And Clara!

- Yes, and Victor.

- Victor, I think I got him, but I have a vague memory. He is same generation than Clara?
- No, a year younger.
- So maybe I had him in 5th grade. Liam is a good boy.
- He's my light. She answers.
- We talked more about Clara.
- How is she? She passes the baccalaureate this year?
- Yes. She is not well, psychologically. She tells me in the process of the conversation that they had lost their father in 2013. The girl still lives it badly.
- Nice to have seen you. Greet Clara from me, if she remembers me.
- Ah yes. She remembers very well.
- Goodbye. Good night. She leaves.

Rather, I receive, Roxane's mother. She is accompanied by her daughter. I start with compliments on attitude and voluntarism. Then I go on to the blockages, and the painstaking work that she does without saying the word. I explain and I see the face of the darkening mom. I resist, I continue. And for a moment I realize that the balance needs to be restored. I would point out that here I am talking about an observation of recent times. But if I judge the whole period, there is a nice evolution. At the beginning, even the will and the behavior were not there. The mother reassures herself of this observation.
- If there is evolution it is good.
- Yes, well, there is a positive development. She must now continue to free herself, ignore her neighborhood and trust herself.
- Yes, that's her problem in other disciplines. She is often afraid.

I then show the copies, and the proof of the evolution between a poorly made drawing, and a diagram completed thanks to persistence. I'm talking about paralysis through fear. She has difficulty in maintaining the will in the search for answers while keeping the hope of finding. The mom seems to get the message perfectly.

Wednesday 04 December 2019

I start the day with the 4th Rome. The session is going well in general, despite some cropping. The principle is that I do not hurry to send all the students to the computers. Once the general instructions are given, I take the time to check everyone's situation before ordering them to change tools or methods. I ignore the waste of time which is not so important. And I no longer make the mistake of returning the copies in the beginning if I want the session to start early and calmly.

Roxane, is more stubborn than usual in an exchange, for a while. I quickly close the conversation. She begins to readily read again without setting herself the goal of answering questions.
- I read all the documents.
- If you don't want to listen to what I say, I withdraw.

I come back a moment later and show her that she must have the three documents in view to use each for other.

I then take advantage of watching Kahina. And she's the one who approaches me. There is another funniest moment with Kahina. She was discreet until the middle of the session. She hands me her copy, well written, with small decorative drawings on the margin. Before taking a copy, I run
- Kahina, I like your positive attitude.
- Smile of Kahina.
I take the sheet.
- It's well written. I'd love to see other Masterpieces like this in the upcoming sessions.
-       Thank you sir.
- Will you go to the computer with Roxane to look for the names of these components?
-       Yes sir.
Other words interfered to enhance the exchange.
- Roxane died laughing.

Thursday 05 December 2019
With 5th Vienna, it's another session without Lisa. I then launch to Nasrine.

- You tell your friend "never go away for technology, even if you are very sick. Because you come in technology and you get healthy". Look, Marie Lise is here, because it's technology.

The concerned girl has a very calm fun.

Victorine and Camilia arrive late. I begin to find Victorine more lovable than her friend. She is more generous in any case. She is the one who picks up the material at the end when the other does not want to do it.

I return the copies. Liam came back with his copy to complain about his grade. He got 16. I explain the cause. I give him the favor to review his work. A moment later he walks around the class room, he does hang gliding or the owl with his scarf. I call out to him.

I speak to him in a discreet voice. His friends don't even understand what my gestures are saying.

- Do you know what I think of you?
-       Yes.
- You must not enter the game of your neighbor on the left. We can have friends. But sometimes if you are not careful, they lead you into deviations and you gradually cross certain limits without realizing it.

\-   Yes I understand.
- You are watched by your comrades. What I say about you must not be different from what your classmates see.

He looks at me then, seems to say "I understand the meaning of the subject perfectly", and I invite him to return to his place. He remained very kind.

Friday 06 December 2019

After two ordinary sixth sessions, I receive the 4th Rome. It's different. I start with Naomi, to whom I ask if she would be exemplary. She answers "yes".
She does just the opposite. She keeps chatting. I change places, she continues, less but could end up disturbing the calm that begins to settle in this table quite positive in the mind of Kahina.

Liam had warned me that Naomi should not be given a positive remark. She would betray. That's what she did. She must have understood when I ignored her by giving the others copies to distribute.

I warn everyone that these last sessions I note the appreciations. So a lot began to participate, like Adriana, Malya, Alia and Joshua.

At 1:30 p.m. I go into the hall to climb the stairs with the 5th Prague class. I meet Jean Marc who says Hello. The blond-haired girl looks down, not knowing if she recognizes the passers-by.

At 4.30pm, I wait in the car for the opportunity to start in front of the students flow. Some greet me, Marco and Adriana.

I see Lana and Zoéline arriving. I ignore them. I also don't know why Lana doesn't pass anymore and don't turn around to say hi, with her friend Clarisse. I'm in no rush to find out. But the resolution is to ignore more people by the way.

The students still do not see the three paintings in the room, apart from the 4th Lisbon, on Liam's remark.

With the new painting in progress, which contains only boys, with only one barely recognizable character, it is possible to change things. And it will continue like this.

The atmosphere with the 5th Prague has returned to normal. I am adamant about changing places. Gwendoline and Janelle are unhappy to switch places.

Florine begins the session now without having listened to the instructions. Her comrade Edwige is always reluctant to listen to reflections. I insist and I come back to the charge more than once, and Florine finally understands that she must clearly identify the image of the component on the Internet and then observe carefully on the gate model before identifying it on the document. She is happy to recognize the infrared receiver and the micro switch. She is happy with her session. Sicilia very kind as she has always been. The boys are less kind. But I'm taking revenge this time. I put on the nicest computers, including Paolo, Rayan the good boy and Sam, and other girls, indifferently groups. And the others stay in their place for document work.

Célia smiled shyly in the hall. In the evening, Charline and Adeline pass by, indifferent.

It is time to think about having no more ties. It's the best way to get connected.

In the teachers' room, I don't say much anymore. Unless small sentences of Small talk with the nicest to break the ice, like began to participate, like Adriana, Malya, Alia and Joshua.

Monday December 9, 2019

I'm leaving the 115 to go to 112, Fernandine looks at me. I'm not waiting to see if she wants to talk to me. I close the door on my way out. Juliette passes, looks at me, her beautiful legendary smile "Hello Sir", "Hello", I pass. I walk along the corridor, all the more long as I meet her former comrades of 5th Varsovie who did not fail to greet me from afar. Claudia G and Manon, and two others I had forgotten, glances conspicuously on the horizon to ignore me. Face closed. Hatred personified. Before them, I meet an elder of the same generation, who was not used to it, but this time she greets me. She is that kind of girl who goes unnoticed. She is ponytail, rather blonde, permanently cold mine.

Leaving the room, Zoéline like everyone else said "goodbye sir", and this time I hear her, she was almost the last. She has a very

shy angel voice. I explained to her the function "to direct" in general. I give back her her copy to see it again.
- "Do not come back at lunch breaks".
- Yes sir. Goodbye
- Goodbye

At 3:35 pm I go down to get the 5th Prague, first group. I couldn't have asked for a better time. At the bottom of the stairs Clarisse looks at me from afar and greets me, and Lana turns around.

I ask if they have technology every Monday. It must be the morning session in my class room. I regret for a while the change of room. I should have waited a little longer before changing rooms.

They are also technology at the last hour Thursday. I then invite them to say hello as they pass.
- It reassures me to see that you are still here....
- Ok. Smiles and laughs.
There were Clementine, Lana and Clarisse.
I get the 5th Prague. They arrive in class. They do not all get in at once, Florine as often last.

Edwige was sad at first. I show that I see it, but I do not intervene.

The turbulent group, Ambrine and Camilia, are slow to get their items out. I move them around so that I have the good guys and the nicest girls nearby, to put them on the model. The session is difficult to get started. They do not leave their business, not very attentive. Some chuckle about the general lack of seriousness. I claim the notebooks of the three girls.

Ambrine asks several times to go to the toilet, then Edene in turn. I make them wait a little, before saying, you were too disrespectful. Go see those you respect better, they can do you some favor. It's a favor, and I don't want to grant you with. You have shown too much hatred and bad spirit. Some words that everyone heard Chained. It was without disturbing the general atmosphere.

I had no intention of refusing them to go to the toilet. But as the session progressed, I began to feel bad about the idea of giving them this advantage. I even heard her comrades who laughed at the ease with which she risked obtaining it.
- So we're not going to go to the toilet?

- No. I respect you and you take that for a weakness.
- Can I go to the computer?
- Not now. First finish the written work.

I make her repeat an evaluation.

Finally only Ambrine G has a double remark as expected in the notebook.

- Why don't the others have any comments? Asks Ambrine
- Because you continued in the provocation.
- She wanted to defend me. Retorts Edene to whom I returned the notebook without notification.
- I just don't like it.

They had nothing more to add.

The good session takes shape gradually. The wiring is done. Florine is often surprised and seemingly hesitant when I ask her. But I do not give in. I continue to involve her more than the others. She must be marked by each of these sessions. She surely is, since she showed enthusiasm for each of her discoveries.

I end up accepting that Ambrine goes to the computer, but alone and far from her friends. I try to positive every gesture. And I reframe every deviation in behavior. The session is smooth.

- Good bye, sir.
- Good bye

With the 5th Vienne, I practically apply the new principle. I'm gradually sending the most deserving to computer. I do not in a hurry to launch a new global activity. I spend the session managing individualities.
- "Lisa is here" Nasrine says me.
I wave with my hand that I am happy to see her again. They are not unhappy with that.

I just received Martin's parents. I don't hesitate to point out his concern for concentration. I no longer give in to over-the-top laxity which prevents me from telling the truth about their children.

Zoéline has just passed with her parents. She turns around twice talking about the technology room or something about.
With the Lands, I proceed by individualization after the general instruction. The principle is never to start with individual cases. Always set a deposit

for everyone. And by the same I isolate the specific cases, which must be seen one by one, by degree of involvement, while monitoring the general atmosphere. Cropping by calling calmly by first names is very effective. They must feel under constant surveillance. By rotating instead of zigzagging, it is possible to respond to everyone's concerns. None have gone to the computer. It would have been unnecessary risk taking.

Not everything is won with Florine. I remind her that she has to return homework late, to review.
- Have you finished them?
- I started them
- Good.

I explain the notion of heat engine to her, she shrugs her shoulders, seems to say "what can it do to me to know?"

I discover Stubborn Octavia when I change her place. I did not give up anything, except on the exchange or I am rather accommodating. It's the way to be wary for the future. I must not let her take up too much space and freedom.

Tuesday December 10, 2019

I go into the teachers' room, I find three colleagues there, Patrice, Viviane the Satanic and Sabia the great. I say hello and no one answers. It's normal, it's friendly.
I see since the Florine class and two of her friends who have just peeking into the room as they pass.

Wednesday December 11, 2019

I'm going to get the 4th Class. I come across a little old one, Victoire. She starts to say a very warm "hello sir". I feel like she is losing weight. A certain Thomas salutes me and tries to clap my hand. I give him a wind and I hear confusion behind. No doubt Louise Marie was looking at him, since I already met her beautiful look, a second rather. It demonstrates one thing. He's someone to put a limit on. I met him in the boxing hall. I nodded to him. The last time I shake him hand. I even exchange a few words with him about the room. He must believe that the invitation is made for endless familiarity.

From the corridor, Charline, another old student, greets me, smiling. I already had students in class room.

At the ten o'clock break, I see Lyna in the dark. She turns around for the second time to say Hello. A moment later, I see Florine passing by, followed by a friend. I do not meet her gaze. She says "hello" quite frankly. I answer. I look, she was already gone.

At 11.15 a.m. I see the 3th Madrid playing sports. Jean Marc is in the middle, with his cap. Students run. Clarisse, Lana and Arthur cheat for a second while walking through the hall. Juliette is absent or does not exercise. I've never seen her play sports.

In the corridor I meet Victoire, Roxane and two other girls, also 6th Brussels class. Roxane looks at me, silent. I think "this is the kind of person who is given a gift, without deserving it". I think back to the June 3D print, which she hadn't even asked for.

Leaving the room, I look at my old sixths in the face. They say "hello" to me. I ostensibly ignore Adeline who is on my right. She calls me "Hello sir". I turn "Hello". – "I don't have space to do" Extended "Adeline".

Maïly from 4th Guatemala, on entering the room, approaches me.
- Did you do these paintings?
-       Yes,
-       They are wonderful
-       Thank you.

Maïly is a nice girl. She gives the impression of being always sad. But she is reliable as a person on a human level.

Nathan G looks at me and greets me "hello sir".

With the 4th Lisbon, the session is very pleasant. They sometimes chat. In the courtyard, I am told that Grégory had put Tatiana a rake. Victorine tells me again in class. I notice that she is sad throughout the session. I don't suggest it but Clara asks me at the end.
- Could Tatiana join us?
-       Yes of course. I was going to suggest it to you.
I can easily get silence after a few seconds. The technique is simple. I ask for "silence" or "your attention". And immediately I pronounce the first names of those concerned. Very quickly I have total silence.

In general, I'm the one who immerses everything in a chat with a necessary joke, or not. An effective session given the volume of content discussed.

With the 5th Pretoria, I place Léon alone with the girls, including Clara. The others are on COMPUTER, alone. They did the wiring. There is efficiency, and pleasure in work.

The session ends in perfume.
- It smells good.
- What is your scent?
- How much do you put in per month?
- What shape of the bottle?

The exchange is longer. They all start at the end of the session to offer perfume brands to find the right one.

In the teachers' room, I discuss with Fabien his motorcycle license. Towards the end of the morning, I come back, I see Edmund Vandruk, a teenager in primarily school. We look at each other, we say hello. He is followed by his father, who answers "hello". We look at each other, I smile. He doesn't. We don't shake hands. I pass my way, too. I had already rather overlooked him when I crossed him in the hall.

Thursday December 12, 2019

The morning with the 5th Vienna, is launched in the ordinary way. My students lack reflex compared to other classes. Lisa and her team mates couldn't find the wiring method until the end.

It was a choice not to direct them directly to the right information but to ask them to search the document. He there may have been a moment of annoyance or frustration in them. But I reassured them at the end by saying that the other groups had done just that. No more. And it was true. They ended up wiring the model but without implementing it. I could have been less harsh on Elya. She is a discreet but very nice girl. They are all organized towards the end. The session went well, since they were confronted with the problem of learning independently.

With 4th Lisbon it's a little different. They come home with a lot of familiarity. I cool them with a wave of the hand to go to their places. They understand, so the tone is given.

During the session, I change places with some, Thomas, Aylan and Edgar. These pupils, who have been warned several times, should no longer be given gifts. I write a remark in Aylan's notebook which allows him to go out into the corridor when I had only called Liam to help me carry the boxes.

This cropping is necessary. I almost killed the relationship with Victoire by refusing for a moment to give her the documents to distribute.

Cropping up on the way she kept her documents and forgetting the notebook were necessary. But it is better to continue speaking in a conciliatory but demanding tone than to ignore it.

At the break, Florine comes with Gwendoline to ask for a document from the previous assignments. She can't find it anymore. I look for it. Then I promise to hand it over to her in the row. It's done.
I go into the staff room. I say hello, Sabia the fat and another do not respond, but Nathalie and another respond.

It is 3:35 p.m. I just finished a painting, that of the cat in the parking lot.
Lana's class passes. I see Clarisse. Nobody calls me. I don't watch them constantly. I don't recognize anyone else except Ilano the redhead.

Friday December 13, 2019
The session with the 6 Oslo is going well. Like Lou's mind. Victory is revealed without consistency. She is may be, angry with Lynda. I ended up bringing her closer to my desk.

With Brussels, there are two assistants who take turns ringing the bell. The first is discreet. It's the blonde Maelis. The second is cumbersome. She has the honor of receiving the tears of Pauline who is crying because I ask to repeat her assessment for the second time, to have a mark higher than 13. The favor was cruel.
- It's well done, I did it with mom.
- The assistant asked me "did you ask her to do this again?" "

I look, I don't answer. I recover, an instant later, the copies in question. I call Pauline at the back of the room to explain the technical functions of the evaluation on the real object.

She does the assessment again. I make her compare at the end with what she had done. She recognizes the gap. But she seems to take it wrong. Never have I taken such a bad job with an assistant. But I resolved not to approach the circle where she operates anymore.

With the 4th Rome class, I notice what Liam warned me, "Not to put a positive remark to Naomi if not she would change badly".

With the 5th Pretoria, the session is pleasant, until Elisa comes to collect Cléandre's notebook. So far everything is correct. But some students start to whisper, and she pats and yells at them. A silence ensues that makes me wait a moment before breaking it, while the supervisor colleague was still there, making the call. The students laugh. I challenge them. Leon Paul retorts. I say "shut up and don't explain anything to me". And silence sets in again.

But I blame it, even if I caught up a bit by intervening almost in time. I take a resolution on the spot. Never greet an invigilator with a usual "hello Madam", which establishes the supervisor's authority in the classroom and her connection to the students. I keep them at the door with an already made absentee ticket, stuck on the door. There makes less interaction. It's what I do Monday and Tuesday. It's very effective. This morning Tuesday I do not even notice the passage of the supervisor. Yesterday with the Vienne, the same Elisa comes back, she must notice, when she asks for those who are absent and I immediately launch out to the pupils "don't answer". I give her the list of absent. She leaves with "Thank you very much Mr. Yohan" I answer "goodbye".

The question is "why do some people think it is weakness when they are given a place and importance.
Friday during the session with the 5th Prague class, I hear a lot of comments on the paintings. At the end of the session, Iris asks
- Did you do these paintings?

\-   Yes.
- Have you done any others?
- Yes, at home, and others in my filing cabinet if you want to see.
I give her the folder but I choose the portraits, I carefully avoid those of her comrades. I show that of Claudia.
- This one is my old student.
She looks and Florine is with her, looks, with a colder air, while Iris is rather smiling.
They're leaving, I don't remember a "goodbye" but I think they said it is their habit.

   Yesterday Monday, going to get group B of the 5th Prague, Iris asked to come. I immediately answer "No". I felt
disappointed her. She turns back to her comrades.
This morning with the 6th Tokyo, I show a certain severity, cropping the comments endlessly from the usual girls, Calypso, Tassiana and Juliette. Fantine is different. She understands better. Even if sometimes I set for her limits in a more courteous way.
I'm writing a Positive note in Olivia's notebook. This is her last technology session

in the establishment. I write that she is the friendliest in the class. And I think so.

This morning I am with the 6th Kiev. Lyna and Florine show up at the door. I make them wait for a moment. Then I signal to get in the class room.
- Bring in, girls.
They hesitate.
- Come here.
They are moving forward a little. None said hello.
-       You want?
-       I lost my .... ..
- I didn't quite hear.

- Look, you have this lost and found box.

For a moment I feel like I'm begging them to do something, like I'm asking.
Florine always looks cold, downcast.
- I think it was during the German session that I forgot it. Add Florine.
- If you need me to open a door for you, you tell me.
I hear neither thanks nor goodbyes. They are leaving. I have an aftertaste that discouraged me practically for a good part of the session. I take again taste when I think

that I have them this afternoon. Florine, still, didn't do her last three home works.

The session resumes, and the wiring activity is a success, since the students find it fun and challenge. I end up finding meaning in what they have to do.

The session ends. Everyone is leaving. I remember that the class of my alumni students usually goes down the hall. I'm standing by the door tidying up. Juliette passes. Her gaze was already sweeping the room.

-       Hello sir.
- Hello Juliette.

Other girls follow her. Look, but without saying a word.

But Juliette alone can wipe out all of the evil spirits of the day. See of the week.

Yesterday Monday, I am in the reserve. A class passes. It's The 5 Prague. I look only once, I meet the gaze of Gwendoline who smiles at me and beams. It's the only. I ignore all the others.

With the Pretoria, Friday, they very keenly notice the paintings. In particular that of the cat whose name they told me.

I just got out of the personalized support gardening session with the Prague. I stayed with Elisa for almost the entire second hour. She is not allowed to use the tools. As the students were motivated, it allowed them to move forward and have fun with woodworking. It is basic but very useful everyday knowledge that they have acquired. The wood saw, the drill, the square, the screwdriver.

Adenise and Julie came greet me. Faïrouz and Nemo would like me to draw them. They like drawing, especially that of the cat.

With the 5th Prague, Florine is very active. She's the one who did the most practice. She's the driving force behind her team.

I make a mistake when I get into the conversation about gifts. By asking Florine the question, she only answers about her father. At first she doesn't mean who gives her a gift. She whispers to her neighbor then she deigns to call me while I was talking with another.
- It was my father who gave me a gift, and all the family.
- In common or separately?
- Separately.

The conversation ends there. It is not difficult to guess that she quoted her mother in the whisper. She shows her evasive interrogative manner with her eyes and her shoulders. Sign of not wanting to answer.

I'm leaving the room since Elisa is having fun talking about the gifts and I'm supervising the operations. I have not gone to see her to plan the activities since the last session. And it is my intention to continue like this. Her habit of telling me about it in the teachers' room, and the first name of the daughter of a colleague who appears in the conversation, annoys me.

I then ask the boys to put away the equipment, "You will finish next time". They are really tired. Rather, it is a successful session, given the content.

A student named Mathis tries to get into the reserve. He is very annoying one, still in 4th grade.

- You have no right.
- I just wanted to ask you something.
- What card to bring back tomorrow.
- The whole binder.
- To find out if....
- I'll tell you. Tomorrow

- Goodbye
- Goodbye

I resolve not to do any more minutes on overtime. No one deserves it outside of school hours. Gone are the days when I was tutoring a certain Claudia S in Géo Gébra. Not a least "thank you". Not a look at the party of the 3rd. The sixth class students that I helped to review, and Taiss who denies that we had agreed on the approach.

For Florine's unreturned homework, I intend not to write appreciations in the end of semester report card. No notes will appear for the period. It will only lower her rating. If she does not do her homework afterwards, the procedure will continue.

Friday morning is the funeral of Stanley Ducat. He died at 18 from a Scooter accident. I will no doubt come across former colleagues, former students from various establishments, but especially those from Saint Martin. I have to look straight and not look people. There is enough disappointment like that.

Friday evening will be a dinner in honor of Madiba's departure. A colleague is watching.

He is a computer scientist. And in the afternoon, it's Christmas market. I will go out to gauge the temperature.

Friday December 18, 2019

I do a session with the 4th Rome, the session is calm. Well managed. I let some chatter go by. Until I install the projection for the desktop computer.

I send some on computer for the discovery of CATIAV5. I don't hesitate to remove Naomi from the computer because she is just chatting. The favorite becomes the plague victim, courteously. She does not protest. I also remove Margot from the computer because she retorts me. Yet she gives me a compliment that I don't understand when she gets in the class room. The session is pleasant. They manage to follow the demonstrations. I find myself wondering if I really have a nice 4th Rome and a 4th Lisbon in the same year.

It's the ten hour break. I'm going to the reserve, I see Lana and Clementine. They go in the same direction. They turn around halfway between the room and the reserve. They are heading towards me.
-   Hello sir.

- Hello. You want to help me carry the boxes.
- Yes.

I give them the boxes of the portal models, for my 5th classes.

- You can put them there. Thank you. You want to see my paintings.
- Ah yes. You made them?
- Yes.

They take the time to look at each table. They focus on that one of the cat, and the other of the workshop.

- It's beautiful they say in substance.

There is moment in the hollow of the wave. The void terrifies me. I then propose the continuation.
- You want to see portraits. Have you seen them? I asked Clementine.
- No.

I hold out the filing cabinet. I put it on the desk. Lana turns the pages. I present Claudia without naming her. Saying it's my old one.
They turn the pages.
- Ah, it's Juliette!
They are still spinning.
- "That sounds familiar ". This is the portrait of Louise Marie.

- Ah, it's Juliette again. She is very beautiful. They are Very well done.
- "It's hard to draw that, turned from behind. You have to stay like that for two or three hours" Said Lana, looking at the scenes of the three old 6th Brussels.
- It's Julie. A fourth, specifies Lana for Clémentine.
- "Who do I see?" Lana asked, laughing. She looks at her portrait. "I was beautiful".
- "You are still beautiful". I answer. She likes the portrait.
- This is on a photo of the 5th. It was the beginning of the year. I have had neither a photo of you since nor one of Juliette.
- You know us, you see us.
- In reality, while drawing, I realized that I hadn't looked at you enough. Even if we see you in class, we don't look at you enough.
- First there are many of you. Then there are limits. It's tricky to watch.
- I see blurry with all this.
- What does that mean?
- It's impressive. That's wonderful.
- Thank you.

It's ringing.
- It was nice to see you again. Come back in the week. Friday, I'm here all day.

- Ok. Thank you, goodbye sir.
-         Goodbye.

I see Lana behind Juliette, entering the gym. It is 10:30 a.m.

At the second break, I go into the teachers' room, I chat with William the computer scientist. He explains to me the sharing on network of personal computers. I chat with Madiba who is going to leave this weekend, retired. We're exchanging the phone.
Before noon I go into the colleague's room. She works on the stairs using graph paper with the 5th Moscow.
- Adeline, what are you doing?
-         A stair.
-         Of the establishment?
-         No!
Adeline is both pleasant at the time and almost amazed that I speak to her.
I finish writing down the schedule and I see Adeline whispering to her neighbor. Not difficult to guess on whom. I go get a box from the back cupboard and leave. Adeline looks at me but I try to ignore her in passing.
I manage to stay disciplined on the call in the morning.

The morning begins with the friendliest girls in the establishment, Lisa, Nasrine and Jana. They're asking to come with the other technology group. I say yes. The session is pleasant, even if the wiring of the model they made has not yet worked. For the others either. I need to check and fix the problem earlier. It turns out that it's just a blockage of the barrier. I have to push it a little.

Madame comes to see me in the teachers' room to ask me if possible not to stay for the entire duration of the funeral, from 8 to 10 o'clock.

I say "I will do my best" to get back in time. I ask that "class 6th Oslo, be in my class room so that I take it when I return". I plan to have this class from 8:15 am to 9:10 am. I would leave it to a supervisor, with a job to do. I get the other class when I get back.

With 4 Lisbon, it's a pleasant session as usual. Victorine seems very happy to be there. She is with Camilia. I take care to place her near me in computers. I have both for the pleasure of the exchange, and also to channel it without rushing it. I can also help her without getting up.

We discover CATIAV5. They had already started it with the colleague. She started a topic. The subject was different from each other, but without a basic introduction.

I then decide to make a common subject. It's modeling of a Smartphone. It seemed to interest the students.

Edgar complains about Liam who turns off his screen. I ask Liam to return to his place. He is not happy, he is not protesting, he remains rather smiling. At the end of the session I call out to him as he leaves.
- Liam, he's coming back.
-         Yes sir?
- You're the boy I said the most about this. And I want to continue doing it. But I'm going to ask you something. And I want you to say yes.
-         What's this?
- Can you be exemplary?
- He won't be able, replied Samuel.
So I put my hand on Liam's shoulder.
- Can you be blameless?
-         "Yes" Replies Liam.
-         It's perfect. Goodbye
-         Good bye, sir.
-         "Yes" replies Liam.

Madame asked that I no longer take pictures of the students, and especially not to show them. It does not bother me that I draw.
I answer that I have not taken photos since the end of last year.
- I happen to take photos, but group photos. The one I took are group photos. And it is during the activity. It's about the end of the year.
- Ok
- Anyway, it's been two months since I have drawn portraits anymore. Students ask me, I answer that I don't do it anymore, and that poses problems. I do college paintings without the students. I took pictures of the school.
- Of course!

She was not rude. I do not insist much. I explain where the idea for these drawings came from. I fail to tell her that these drawings are an act that I do not intend to regret.

Friday December 20, 2019.

I bring the 6th Oslo. I do a wiring scssion with them. I don't turn on any computer, not even mine. The session is pleasant. I warn me that I will leave them at 9:10 am. A boy asks me the reason, and I explain that it is to go to the funeral of one of my former sixth graders, now in terminal. They seem to know a little. It happened on local television. They do not yet know the Scooter. They describe it a bit.

When I announce that I leave at 9:10 am, and that they will be permanently the rest of the session, they express a joy that surprises me. I'm not that used to the sixth content of not seeing myself.

I enter the church. It was rather towards the end. I regret having agreed to leave school only at 9.10 am. It's too much concession. But Madame did not want me to attend the funeral for the full two hours. I have to remember.

I meet well-known faces. I am surprised not to see many students from his old Sainte-Marie schools. I think recognizing Laurine F. Always so beautiful in tears. Most are alumni of Saint Etienne School. I recognize Louise, Lina, Anissa, Sarah, Clémentine, Clémentine. I find myself at the end near the entrance with Bernadette, the French colleague at the Lycée. I see Célia Stanislav coming from far away. Approaching, I think ... Finally she comes to give a big hug to a friend, then another. I'm waiting. Then she arrives at Bernadette. Madam ... she kisses her. Then towards me, Sir... she kisses me. I do not fail to show her a natural affection, in memory of the good old days and circumstances, with one hand behind his back. What the colleague does not fail to notice.

On entering, Arthur comes to greet me. He was with someone I barely recognize.
I greet Perrine with my eyes. Nadège comes to approach me. She rises up to me for a little while, as if not to leave me alone. The chairs on this right side of the aisle are emptying.

Margaux Gad, always faithful, looks at me and greets me with eyes. I recognize Clara. and many others whom I will not name and who sometimes ostensibly ignore me.

Louise looks at me more than once, a moment when she leaves, she whispers to her neighbor. It's easy to guess the subject.

Girls are in tears. Sophie is coming out in tears when I come back.
It's easier to recognize girls than boys.
I'm coming back to class. The 6th Brussels do not seem very happy to see me again. They look happier in the on-call session.
I receive the Prague at 1:30 p.m. They are no more pleasant than usual. It's the most unpleasant class of the week. Curiously, Florine is the nicest. She comes to see me several times. She comes first, to give me a late homework. And come again to ask to postpone some homework. I leave her the choice between doing it immediately or after the holidays. She makes the easiest choice.
Even Sicilia I catch her typing with her pen on the keyboard in order to cause an annoyance. It was successful, but I do not show it. I avoid her gaze. I leave time. At the end she asks to go in her place instead of continuing to work on 3D software. It's no longer a luxury. It will therefore be necessary to make an austere plan. Make it desirable.

I put three words in the notebooks, Edene, Cléandre and August. They thought they were getting out. Cléandre tries, when he sees me taking his notebook, to distract me by anticipating the functions that I am about to explain. He realizes that he did not know. And that he cannot distract me from writing a word in his notebook. No more courtesy I had for August in honor of his very kind sister. She, and her pampered friends, says no longer hello to me since the last year.
So I can't totally ignore Florine. But I'm not going to speak to her directly. I only say her friend's first name and I don't look at her when she says hello when I get home.
But she does not fail to say "goodbye" and "good vacation".

The session with the 5th Pretoria is talkative but no bad spirit apart from Venissia's permanent annoyance. She is no longer smiling as before. After the holidays I'm going to have to ignore her a bit and stop joking about her to keep her from talking. No more familiarity.

I allow myself to play the guitar in the last ten minutes of the session. Leon is full of praise.
- Sir, you're top with the guitar.

The 5th Tirana class student's are very calm. Louise is the spirit of this class. She's the nicest girl maybe of all the fifth. Kind, attentive, very dignified, accessible to the ambient humor and very beautiful.

Leaving the establishment at 4.30 p.m., near the gate, I stop for a moment due to congestion. I cast a furtive glance on the pupils, without fixing a second Lana. I perceive her presence with her blue parka. She turns to me. I looked ahead. She said nothing. She was in 5th Varsovie two years ago. It was the kindest class. The girls were in competition with each other, but nothing bad. They were almost all funny. Before Christmas a certain Coline arrives. She was coming from public School. Integrate this class, and disintegrate it. Clans are formed. First Claudia walks away from Janna. Towards the end Célia moves away from Juliette and Clarisse. The following year, from the middle of the year, Juliette was no longer a girlfriend with Lana and Clarisse. Coline is still Juliette's turn to make her and defeat her group of friends according to the mood. It was a sickly jealousy with Hatred to the fullest. The day she accompanied her to class not so long ago, she had three years of being together, when it was not two years ago.

At 6 p.m. it's the departure evening of colleague Madiba. I see colleagues I haven't seen in a while, as Laurence. We discuss. But I'm a bit hungry. I find her wait-and-see. It doesn't fuel much conversation. She listens, she reacts. I'm talking to her about literature. She's not trendy enough for an English teacher. I chat with Ségolène, Taiss D and Eden. It's more pleasant and interesting, often funny.

Diana takes pleasure in letting me see her travel album published in books. But she doesn't have time to sit down and chat. When she left, she cuddled the big cat. I call her. She comes to my car then I show her the painting of the cat.

- You are an artist. Well done. She was not pretending.

- Thank you.

I chat for a while with a German, Catherine's companion. He is the former German teacher.

I chat a lot with Sabia C, about the links I have or don't have with the staff room. She always has the idea that I have to come more often and mingle with others.

Catherine V kisses me and wishes me happy holidays before leaving, with conviction. Emilie greets me before leaving, but while continuing to chat with Catherine D. Do not even pronounce my first name, and do not look me in the eyes. I have the same impression with Odeline L.

Geraldine is the only one with whom I had nothing during the evening, neither on arrival nor on departure. While, companion Chris, whom I hadn't noticed, reaches out to greet me.

With Anthony I have a long conversation about identity, the popular movement in the south of the Mediterranean.

The supervisors and other staff are all very friendly, Laurence, Obryan, Damien and Taiss.

I meet Gwenn and Elise in the evening. They come to me at the end of the ceremony, they are happy to see each other again.
- Are you staying for a drink?
- No, we have to leave. We have a bus to take.
- I won't hold you any longer then.
- We will come back in February.
- Come and say hello. My class room is 112, the door is always open.
- Goodbye, good holiday
- Goodbye, happy holidays

Thursday January 2, 2020

I'm going to Decathlon to buy a shaker. When I get to the cash desk, I run into Célia Stanislav.
- You are here for a short period or it is final.
- I'm here for a two-month internship.
-      For your studies? What are you doing? I haven't heard from you in a while!
- I am studying sport in a school in Lille. So I have to do an internship in sports equipment.
- In Lille USTL university?

- No, it's a school near Cormontaigne…!

- I know. It's the way towards Saint Philibert.

- Yes
- I introduce my card?
- Just a moment. Do you have a loyalty card?
- Yes, I'm always loyal to Decathlon.
- Smile.
- I'm glad to see you here.
-       Me too
- Good evening, and happy New Year.
- To you too sir.

Monday January 6, 2019

It's back to school. In the car park, I managed to park without disturbing anyone in time. It's the first resolution of the year. I come across Odeline L, Rachelle and an assistant. The latter is the warmest. The other two I feel obliged to greet me.

I go down to the teachers' room, I find Elisa. We are talking about the Mayor and his funeral. She knew his parents.

I compliment Anthony on his elegant look. He has less hair and hair. He seems to like it.

Mélinda arrives. She had cut off contact with me up to the painted picture posted on the internet. She had complimented well. She renews the compliments indoors. I'm going to see Odeline for pay slips. I'm back in the teacher's room. We discuss, Mélinda,

Laura and me, the Ensap account that must be created to have the pay slip. Marie Cecile gets in. I am closest to the door. She greets everyone. I turn. She kisses me, "best wishes" smiling.

She's on tour. She enters the conversation. She is pleasant and humble. She is always frank about her shortcomings and flaws. It makes her charm in addition to the rest.

I soon leave the room. I'm going to see Obryan to ask for the power to be turned back on in room 112. I have just realized that I am badly expressed. I should say room 113. He replies that Damien can now put it back. He did training. But I have to go see him again to rectify my request. It's good he came, Damien. He turned the power back on. We discussed the gardening project.

The session with the 6th Dublin and Tripoli, including Zoéline and Janna Flory, is pleasant. I leave room 115. I see my old ones arriving. Fernandine, and two other girls don't say hello. One of them is unknown, and Juliette, all radiant. Juliette says hello first, I answer "hello and best wishes". She responds "best wishes". And Fernandine also responds "best wishes to you too". The other two continue to wonder if they are at the right door or it is in the other class room.

The most important is Juliette. She is smiling, happy and pleasant.

This is the second good news of the day at the establishment, after Marie Cecile.

I meet Christian James in the corridor who ignores me. Behind him Emilie who comes forward to greet me.

- Hi, best wishes.
- Best Wishes, Happiness and health.

By bringing back the 5th Prague, I meet Vandruk, hands in pockets. He is in effeminate look. He glances perhaps with an intention to say hello. I don't know if he says anything. At the same time I confuse the message with an expeditious "happy new year". There is nothing more.

The two afternoon 5th sessions go off without a hitch. They are all nice. The last with the first group of 5 Prague begins in an exhausting way, bay a chat because of the places. I post the "best wishes" they are all pleasantly surprised. They also respond. But at the end of the thirteenth minute I make the remark. I ask several times to sit down and open the filing cabinet, and the reaction is not very visible. They understand the importance of the remark. The rest is more pleasant, even if I am more severe with some. Florine is more kind. She participates better than all. I make a remark to her neighbor when they are both distracted. But Florine knows how to receive the message.

Tuesday 07 January 2020.

This morning with the 6th Tokyo students are as talkative as before the holidays. I'm not giving up anything. I crop in a calm and subtle way without any familiarity. Fantine remains almost flawless. She understands the promotion from which she benefits.

I go into the teachers' room, I say hello. Cannelle, Odeline L and Elisa respond. I find them warmer than before the holidays.

At 11:15 am, the 3rd Madrid passes. I see Clarisse and Lana passing by, almost fleeting. Avoid stopping almost conspicuously.

I'm thinking of the 5 Prague. Most of them are going to snow class next week. So I will see them to choose the seeds to make, to order while waiting for their return.

I come into room 05, they are with Elisa. Only Augustine gets up. Madame doesn't ask them. This is one thing to remember. It is not easy to return the favor. In any case for her, I will refuse to the students to get up. I'm going for it.

- As you are leaving next week, I come to ask you to come up with seed ideas, by team.

As I explain, I open the filing cabinet, and the groups from Sicilia and Camilia, see the drawings. They start to laugh discreetly whispering. There is nothing unpleasant.

- We will make the seeds as we go, answers Elisa.

She vaguely explains the periods. Except that with her, nothing is ever clear until the end of D-Day.

- We are not going to sow everything at the same time, but we are going to order everything at the same time.
- Absolutely, she joined me.
- "I'm not going back without anything. I give these sheets, in a group, you will offer me ideas. With Madame, you are going to adjust the periods for each seed. She controls the calendar better than I do".
- "Come on, put yourself in a group", enjoins the colleague.

Students get into groups and suggest ideas on paper. They pass one after the other on the board to present. I found Maxence and Florine particularly interesting.

I have the opportunity to observe Florine speaking without being the central character.

I had never found her so radiant. I'm looking to direct and reframe students for more attention. The session ends.

- They played the game,
- Yes, absolutely, answers Elisa.

The session was pleasant. Elisa stays professional and friendly. She knew how to adapt to my proposal despite these previous choices.

Wednesday 08 January 2019

In the teachers' room, I chat with Fabien. One more, who falls with short arms on Madame, who had just "rounded up" all the cups and spoons because they are never washed by their users.

He then recounts the lack of recognition for all the thankless tasks he performs, for a supervisor's salary. Transport equipment, repair equipment and monitor. He explains

to me that on "sick" days it is better to take them during the leave. He was injured once, he was told not to mention that he was carrying equipment on the stairs because he had neither the right nor, above all, the duty. I go back to the class room.
Edmon Canal calls me down the hall.
- "Mister are you coming tonight" to boxing?
- Yes I will resume this evening
- Me too I resume.

I continue on my way. He hadn't spoken to me since the last year, while he often sees me in the hallway, eyes meet. While his father, never fails to greet me in the boxing gym.

January 9, 2020

I'll get the 5 Vienna. Nasrine, Lisa and Jana ask to be able to go constantly instead of going to technology, replacing the last session. I propose to come in technology and do permanence. It enchants them better than their proposal. This is the main. I take advantage then, it couldn't be better, to have them correct their assessments to increase the score.

I warn that the session will take place in two stages, first on the computer then on the

model. I pulled myself together part time. I review my ambitions. It is better to do one activity, to devote yourself fully to it. And finish it. What I do. Half of the students understood the meaning of the instruction and the way, even if no one finished.
With the 4 Lisbon, the session is pleasant. Clara is true to herself, serious, fast and attentive.

Victorine and Camilia are always pleasant and hilarious as usual. I call Camilia.
- We are going to establish a contract between me and you.

- Smile hesitation.

- Not with my person! It shouldn't be confusing. You've been in my classes for two and a half years. ...Victorine died of laughter. She goes out into the hallway to breathe. ...
- I would like you to participate during this semester which starts at the weekend.
-        Yes
- The hardest part is doing the exercise of raising your hand.
-        Yes I know.
- You have to get used to it. Raise your hand to say anything. Search the wordbook for a random word and use it.

- "Yes"...Camilia smiles.
- Then the next step, every time I ask a question, ask yourself" where is the answer?" to the blackboard? Look in the folder? Search in your culture? ...
-      Yes. Camilia smiles, and almost laughs, and Victorine is still Laughing.
- Ok, that's perfect.

She returns to her place. During the session I didn't stop asking for Clara and Victorine's help. She is closest to the office, but not only.

I end up placing everyone on the computer, and sending a few to their places, for behavior.

Most of them, especially Igor and Victorine, are disappointed that I am not picking up the job. I explain but I feel that it does not pass.

I return to the room for the next session. They are with my colleague. I claim the documents. They are happy that I do it.

At the break, I meet Gwendoline and Florine in the corridor. They say "hello sir" with a smile. I say "hello".

It is 3:20 p.m. Gabrielle and Elene greet me after leaving the technology class.

It is 3:42 p.m. The 3rd Madrid class students are entering the technology room with my colleague. Juliette turns, I watch at the right time.
- "Hello sir" She said, joining the salute with her left hand,
- Hello Juliette.
Lisa, Jana and Nasrine pass out. They find me in the car.
- "Good bye sir" Say they very warmly.

- Goodbye.

Fernandine accompanied by Feryel and Juliette camouflaged in her hood, pass discreetly, in the rain which begins to fall.
Alessia makes a double goodbye without specifying to whom. I don't answer.
The usual Fantine, Calypso and Tassiana launch a triple goodbye all along the route.

Monday January 13, 2020
The session of the 6th takes place without the slightest annoyance in room 115. An interesting participation and exchanges on the rocket and energies in general feed the session. Small jokes are possible on Janna's teddy bear. We leave to go to room 112.

In the other room, I have to give instructions several times to go out and open the notebooks. Including for serious students like Janna, Zoéline and Victor. The annoyance goes up a notch.

Janna always speaks in the same tone. Instead of answering questions, she makes comments, sometimes even interrupting the explanation of the instructions. When I explain the type of wiring done in series, and the one to be done in parallel, she allows herself to say "so what." Zoéline looks at her embarrassed and amused.

I pretend not to hear. I keep going but I realize that I have to lower my tone and I control my nerves and theirs again.

Clementine asks me if there is a way to have a charged battery. I explain that we must first apply the current set point. I see her a moment later discouraged, disillusioned. I jostle her courteously to revive her. Then she finds a commercial smile.

After a while, I sense that the weariness is likely to settle quickly. I then decide to stop the activity and send them to computer to start the homework on vehicle energies. They are relieved. I then promise Clementine to give the next time charged batteries.

The waste of time gives me the idea to review the idea of this change of room. Especially since Obryan had offered me the possibility of going back on my choice.

The afternoon session with the 5th Prague begins with too much gossip and a touch of annoyance. This is often the case when there is an aside at the start of the session. These are the three; Iris, Elisa and Angelina asking where to sit, I should have made them wait.

I decide to pick up the homework and do an evaluation. This makes it possible to rush things. I do the restitution and the evaluation in the same activity. It is understood that at least the good half understands programming according to a given code, like Arduino.

I give the same homework to finish for everyone. This benefits those who have not gone skiing.

The session is quite effective with the 5th Vienne and the 5th Tirana. In the parking lot, Sandrine makes me think.
- You should warn those you annoy with your vehicle.
- But I don't recognize the vehicles!
- You go to the teachers' room
- Yes, I should warn, with a sarcastic tone.

I shorten the conversation and go away. I don't find it useful to show my annoyance. She must surely perceive it. I think back to my resolution to arrive on time, around 7.40 am. I'm just waiting for someone to think about me, to react to the people who park two out of three places. As well as on the ground markings still awaited.

Tuesday January 14, 2020
It is 3:20 p.m., three girls show up outside the door. It's Charline, Victoire and Galiane. They return, hesitantly, for fear of disturbing me. They approach the office.
- Hello sir
- Hello girls
- We haven't been here for a long time, because our French teacher puts us a lot of hours and changes our schedule.

"Sometimes we don't even have time to eat", justifies Victoire and Charline.
- Who is your French teacher?

- Madame Bourbon.

- The problem with her is that she doesn't have much authority, adds Galiane. It warns but it does not sanction.
- ... ..
- You are the one who paint?
- Yes
- Either way it's your style
- You are fine?
- Not always. I'm a little bit stressed
- On what?
- On many things, as my daughter among others.
- We have no authority and we stress. When you have a daughter, I don't even speak. I wouldn't imagine having a responsibility like that.

... ..
- I'm telling you a secret. The class that annoys me the most is that of your former comrades.
- The 5th Prague? Check one.
- Especially Pierre, he tampers with tickets... remembers Victoire

I do not insist on the subject. It just rang...
- You can't know how nice it is to see you again. I'm not holding you back any longer.
-         Good bye, sir
-         Goodbye. See you soon

Wednesday January 15, 2020

I ask Obryan down the hall if he doesn't mind going back to the system before. That with his third, he goes to 112 instead of 115. I explain how the change of room wastes too much time with the students who take time to go out of items again. He smiles and understands. He is as usual helpful and courteous.

At the council of 6th Oslo, during the student report, Siham noted that I only interviewed girls. It shocked at first. Then she corrects by specifying.
- He only questions students who do not raise their hands.
- Ah! That's it! Yes.... Laugh the colleagues and Madame.

During the Dublin Council, Taiss gives "Praise" to three girls, for essentially "their smiles" Among others.

I even point it out to her once, she laughs. But Madame who does not laugh seems even to be wary that I take note of it.

The third council is that of the 6th Kiev. Opposite is Marie Cecile.

We sometimes look at each other. But more often I avoid meeting her gaze.

At the end, she makes her intervention last.

I hardly see any negative point. Well Named. There is no negative point either. But she takes it upon herself.

We meet in the teachers' room. The conversation takes hold. She takes it hard to say that it was bad with two boys in particular. It's Ethan, whom I have in class, and a certain Igor.

The exchange in advice on the latter is long. It poses problems.

- He's endearing. We want to get him out of there. Taiss begins.

- "He is endearing. He has a good head. We want to help him" adds a student mom.

The conversation continues between Marie Cecile, the kind music teacher and me. We are on the same wavelengths.

- We are a little too much.... Begins Marie Cecile

- "Too nice" ... added I.

- Yes, agrees Marie Cecile.
- I have the impression that some tenured professors are trying at all costs to wrest "praise" too easily.
- Yes, adds Carole laughing.

We discuss another 10 or 15 minutes in the parking lot. And we take leave. It's already very dark, almost 8 pm.

Thursday January 16, 2020.

I start a new, simpler sequence than the previous one with the 5th class. Construction bricks to make walls, then vaults.

Only one group succeeds in their vault building in each of the two classes. The disappointment of Louise, the nicest of girls, is great. I promise to erase it without telling him next time. I regret not being present enough with her group. I had an idea for myself the year last. It is to make one group succeed each time in its activity and preferably the most serious group. To be sure you can go to the synthesis.

I notice the bad mood throughout Octavia and Clara's session. They seem to have been unhappy since the start of the year, even more today that I removed Hélène from their table. Neighborhood and friends are important to the students. Leaving, Clara says goodbye, but not Octavia.

I begin work on the book of evaluations. Looking at the mass of documents available, I realize that it is doable. And it's urgent to start it.

As I sort through the documents, I hear the loud voice of Patricia SVT, who is shouting. She does not stop mixing course explanation, instructions, reminders to order, and morals to decorate everything, in the same tone. So she doesn't stop talking during the session out loud.

We over-saturate the space in front of our students with our words. You have to let the student's mind breathe.

When a teacher says an interesting sentence, he admires himself. He then decides to continue to listen even better. When he should just say a nice sentence and then shut up.

I go down to give Odeline the greeting card, I ask her
- Is there any point?

- Eh yes!
- Do they stop at your level or do they continue?
- I order them and transfer them.
- I was wondering, that's why I was a little late. OK, thanks.
- Goodbye.

To make photocopies, I find Patricia doing hers. She always responds aggressively, "I'm not done", I don't stay in the cabin. She pumps the air.
I go out to greet Taiss, and chat with. But I promise to crop it one day, but I prefer that colleagues be present.

I ask Alfred once the reason for her permanent bad mood. He replies, "She is badly fu... "

In the teachers' room, I come in, I say hello. I hear hello, they all respond, Emilie, Laurent, school assistant and Marie Cecile.
It is 1:39 pm when a third class takes place in the technology room. Taiss Vierra wakes me up from my concentration on the computer with a "hello sir". A wave of the hand and a very warm smile interfere. She seems to be called to order by her teacher.

This is not the case for the other students who cry.

It is 3:42 p.m., the black mambas follow each other. The little one is behind the big ones. They tour on the other side, listening to a great nothing that speaks and says nothing.

Monday January 20, 2020.

I return to room 115 for the 6th Tripoli and Dublin. In the teachers' room, Mélinda renews the compliment "I didn't know you were an artist". With the 5th, I rotate places in the different tables. I'm doing a brick vault building session with the 5 Prague. It's Florine's group. None succeeded, despite all the seriousness of Paolo and Rayan. Iris intends to return seriously. She smiles less, she is more attentive.

I propose to Florine "the promise" or "the contract" to obtain "Praise" in June. I tell her that only a few can hope for it. Sicilia, Paolo, the twin sisters can be but not sure. Camilia is not sure either.
- You have to be flawless. You are often great in class, but sometimes there are empty passages. She seems interested in the idea.

At the end of the session, she came to tell me that she had installed Arduino on her computer. I'll explain the technique a bit. I then move on.
- If you want to come and train here, and I'll let you do the wiring, but you're the one who decides to come, I won't ask you.
- She nods timidly
She comes back to the idea,
- And what did you tell me? I did not understand.
- I'll write to you to explain.
I go out quickly and I let Florine and Edwige pull the door.

The class council is going as planned, stressful and unpleasant. The most comforting thing is that the majority of teachers have the same feeling as in technology. I took care to avoid intervening first in order to see. Odeline, Carole Bourbon, Patricia, Martine, say the same thing. It's a talkative and painful class. Only the mother of the delegate Sicilia defended tooth and nail the students individually and collectively. She knows how to pass colleagues off as bad guys.

The only difficulty students noted with technology was the insufficient explanation of the exercises, especially software.

I readily admit. It makes colleagues laugh. Then I explain that I planned them. "You will do, without understanding everything from the start, and you will learn by doing." It amuses Sicilia a little, and also probably her mom, on whom she looked when I spoke. The moment is rather fun for everyone.

But bitterness remained. I take revenge on the second, with the Pretoria, or I only do the subjective. I emphasize the possibility of applying a differentiated pedagogy. The class is nice. I'm not exaggerating anything.

Christian and Marie Dax notice that I note everything. I take pleasure in noting the consensus majority in this Prague council. It's a kind of overwhelming animism. The unique thought denounced by Marie Cecile.

Tuesday January 21, 2020

I engage the students in a computer activity after a video clip, in order to replace the animated sites. So much the better, they will learn how to do word processing in Word. They are not unhappy. Room 115 is more like a computer room than a technology room. I thus understand Obryan's choice to purify his room. It's much less tiring, and less messy.

I take the opportunity when I see two boys who were making misery for Marie Cecile, having fun on computer. I send them back to their place. I also crop them when they offer to help me with the material.

The resolution is to stop trying to see the elders. Those who come are welcome. 3D printing gifts as a souvenir of the good old days are over. And the same rule must apply in the city.

New momentum is needed for the second semester

Odeline refuses to change the photo. "I don't have time," she replies. If someone doesn't want to be on the brochure, you don't have to be on the photo. If I do that, it doesn't end.
- Thank you goodbye.

Adeline takes pleasure in being of service, to move the bin. She said "goodbye" with her beaming smile.
Clara whispers with Heloise. It remains to be seen what.
- Clara!
-        Yes?
-        I do not say anything.
For the first time, I take the time to take stock and the interest of doing so, with the 4th Lisbon. I take the time to recall the basics of automation and to clearly distinguish between inputs and outputs, orally. They will copy the balance sheet next time.
I withdraw Cléandre from his team because he disturbs his comrades who build a brick vault. I request that he prepare his workbook for verification. I end up asking him for help to cut and glue pieces of wood and glue them to make a keystone. He feels useful. But this freedom gives him back his primitive instinct, which strikes Loana "without paying attention" with scissors, injuring her hand.

I did a sequence of automatism with the 5th before launching on the 4th. I started it when my colleagues were on duty because they didn't have a computer. However, I take more time to explain how it works with the 4th ones. But one of the lessons learned from experience. Students in the 5th grade act as gentle guinea pigs with this sequence.

The most recent resolution is to free up time, in order to be able to think about the career in general. I have also to bring a hint of rigor to the organization of the sequences.

From the start of the session with the Pretoria, I give a rant. I instruct you to open the filing cabinet and write the beginning of the sequence. Zoéline and Naomi wait and watch. I shoot a sentence. And I keep calm. It is necessary and effective.

Monday January 27, 2020

In the hall I meet Damien. That's good. I was going to see him to follow the order of seeds and gardening's equipment.
- Any news from you?
- "Yes", laugh.
- The order, were you able to place it?
- I'm waiting for a call. Let madam give permission too.
- What is right?

- Jean Marc from the Lycée. He must be available to pick up the equipment.
- When can you call him?
- I'm going to call him later.
- You hold me informed?
- Okay, I'm here to tell you about it.
- Ok, thank you, I'm in the reserve.

Less than an hour later, Damien shows up at the reserve.
- It's okay, I called. At 2 p.m. I will go get the equipment.
- It's perfect. I'm in the room. As soon as you receive it, you can move on. I have students but the door is open.

At 2:30 p.m. Damien arrives with panoply of seed bags and a kind of agrarian calendar.

If I had not gone to see him, and if I had not insisted on my disappointment that he was not already delivered, things would stagnate. It was no longer useful to go to Elisa. Because at the moment she is only managing ideas but nothing concrete. She has good gardening skills, but the students are at risk of getting bogged down.

I run the session with the 6th Dublin and Tripoli. I start to distribute the material as motion transmission models. And gradually

I feel some students not very serious, not very relevant, as Clémentine Bonbon and Janna Flory. The latter does not stop asking me questions off topic.
- I lost my canteen card from the row.
- I advise you to tell the supervisor Mrs. Elisa. Do you know who it is?
- Yes the one with black hair.
- Or, Mister Fernand
- Ah, not him.

- But I advise you to go alone. And tell him about it.

I begin to find the group of Clémentine, Victoire and Janna not very concentrated. They are a little seriousness in the investigation. I notice that they start to have an influence on Zoéline who was exemplary until then.

I then decide to write him a note. Louise discreetly transmits it to him. She will read it at the back of the room. She answers me in writing on my request. "I will do my best ".
I stop the activity 15 minutes before the end. First I take stock of the lack of seriousness of some. But I only cite the

names of those who deserve "Praise" for behavior. I omit to quote Zoéline. I cite many others. It's an answer to Janna's question.
- How to get "Praise"? What grade is it from?
- We have sometimes given "Praise" to a student who was 15. She is in high school now. I think of Cassandra. But she was exemplary in attitude. She makes never untimely intervention. Don't bother anyone. No one has influence over her.

Everyone says "goodbye", except Clementine who looks at me for a moment while leaving the room without saying anything, shows a frozen smile.

In the afternoon, I end up having an efficient and pleasant session with the 5 Vienne. It's caught in the last quarter of an hour on a signal from Lisa. I move on to the most important question. Students look for a solution on the beams. Vertical section retained. I save the session thanks to the eye gesture of Lisa that she addresses to Clementine and Jana. Signifying that the session is starting to be heavy or long, or something like that.

With the 5th Tirana, for once I feel annoyed because of the chatter, and also for Rose's bad mood. The groan of Clara and Octavia becomes too obvious. I take from the latter an SVT notebook which she copies. Ditto for Salomé. I rip resource copies. That's English. I hear "it can't be done".

I take stock of the chat calmly. I name the concerned ones and I underline what is annoying, gossip, laughter and inappropriate behavior.

It's ringing. It's the break. The students leave the room. There remains Axel and Anthony. Axel doesn't stop chatting instead of putting away his things. I take his things and put them down in the hallway. Surprised but persuaded.

Leon returns. He hands me his obviously well done flowchart, and his written response. He takes leave smiling. I enjoy reading his word. He's the best of the year, since he's "touched" by my text.

The session with the Sicilia group is going very well. All the serious students managed to build the vault.

The Council of 4th Rome is the most pleasant of the year as it is the least hypocritical.
At 1:20 pm I make photocopies. Juliette appears. Look at me and say
- Hello.
- Hello.

She is followed by Coline. She is a rascal and cold one, who does not even look. I keep thinking of passing the message to her that this is the worst dating she has had among girls. For boys I still prefer to be silent.

At 5 p.m., I go down for the council. I fall at the bottom of the stairs on Lana.
- Hello sir.
- Hello Lana.
It was after a long break. She has the best attendance and a more central and more faithful environment than Juliette.

Tuesday January 28, 2020
Calypso is in a bad mood during the almost all the session. I write her a note on paper. She replies "because Tassiana kicked me out of my place". But also "because we haven't worked on computers today".

It is 9:50 a.m. Obryan the educational senior advisor and Madame show up in the class room for a little minute. I had learned the lesson. I shake hands with Obryan and a bow to the other.
The Lynda Victoire case continues.
- We have a problem with kids in sixth grade. To whom you wrote a note on paper.
- I always have the word on paper.
- No, I have it. Answer madam.
- So this is the first one you have. The one I wrote. I have Victoire's answer.
- It can be misinterpreted. You must no longer write. You have to go see the head teacher, because it happened outside the classroom.
- No, it happened in my class. A student comes to see me that another student would have called her....
- At that time you have to write this in the notebook.
- No, I don't write that in the notebook. Especially not before knowing where the problem begins. I don't like scandal. I prefer that the session continues calmly.
- "So you have to see the students at the end of the session" suggests Obryan.

- You don't think what you say! There is no frame here that allows me the teacher to see the students outside of class.

We often say that in meetings, assemblies. We're here for the students. But apart from the course, there is nothing that allows it.
The two are embarrassed to have contradicted each other. The face changes color.

- You receive them downstairs, in the offices.

You have to have time.
- I know it's not written here. But I've been doing it for a while. And that solves problems.
I then cite some of the previous cases.
- We do, retorts Madame D. I sometimes have students in class. I say to write down what they feel.
- I don't know what is causing you a problem. Is it the fact that the management is not aware of it or that I write to my students?
- It's writing to the students. I understood this when, after several written exchanges with students, a student began the letter with "Mom". There I said stop.
- It doesn't happen here. I add.

- I've never heard of that.
- I heard about that. It is done elsewhere. I learned this from the most famous French teacher of our time.
- Who is it?
- Patrice Meirieu. I know he is not liked ... I was going to say the French right. But I hold back. ...he is not loved by everyone. I regret having hesitated at the time.
They both seem to not know him.
- In any case, we are there to manage this kind of problem. You go back to the homeroom teacher or to Obryan. They are the ones who manage this.
- Okay.
- Here is. Thank you. Good luck.
- Thank you goodbye.

I had deleted the concept of the main teacher outside the board, in my practices. This time, it's forever. No more teachers will receive information from me about concerns between students.

It is 12:30 p.m. Alia goes back to class, alone, with her glasses.
- Do you know how to fix my glasses?
- They are twisted from the three joints. I'm going to try.

I do my best with pliers. She is not unhappy with the result.

I wonder then, what would be my reaction if Madame saw that. No doubt explosive and uncompromising on my part.

In the afternoon, the session is more interesting. I am reassured as long as there is equipment, a bin and seeds.

I spend the session calculating the number of bags of soil required. The pupils are sometimes talkative, without being unbearable. The distributed and the state of mind installed, allowed to have exchanges sometimes funny and often relevant. A few dangerous phrases punctuated the duration.
- Florine, you're going to sit down and write down.
- Can't I stay there?
- If you stay there, we will only look at you.
The embarrassment is felt and laughter restrained.

- Sicilia, instead of Janelle I would be upset. You just turn your back on it!
- "She wants to watch August". She is in love, explain Marie.

I look at August. I had never found him so beautiful. I don't want to say it right away. I study the rest of the conversation on the subject.
- Iris is beautiful. Said Florine
- I have no right to say it, but I have the right to think so.
Again surprised and amused.

Damien comes in, staying very tactile and bent over his screen. This is, with no doubt, his way of relieving stress. It's an easy introduction. While he remains attentive to the awkward and curious questions of the students.

He appreciates the work of calculation, of which he sees the last unfolding. He himself confirms the number of bags, which I did not know until then.

Elisa comes in a long time after the ring. It takes the merit of showing the lunar calendar that I had brought back. But I do not see any clumsiness there. Students clearly see that there is no competition between the two. But we show perfect complementarities.

The chatty girls had asked to go out a little before the end. I make them wait and then I refuse. Elisa also refuses. The sanction is there.

I leave the room fairly quickly. I don't want to second or saturate the space anymore. You have to be useful or absent.

Wednesday January 29, 2020.

The session of the 4th Rome begins more sympathetically than it ends. I start with everyone. I finish with a few some. I take three notebooks and I don't return them at the end of the session.
Students ask me.
- I'm not giving them back now.
- When will it be?
- I do not know. This conversation is over.
- Can I ask you something? Add one of the three.
- No, I don't answer. You go out.
But I keep calm the rest of the session. I'm lucky to have a deep voice today. That allows me to impose myself effortlessly. So sometimes I have calm and sometimes localizable chatter. I am happy to put negative features on the copies. It allows me to have a sequenced calm.

I go into the teachers' room. I find Sabia R almost alone and a supervisor still unknown. I accost the colleague. It is a kiss.
- So Yohan, how are you?
- I try to hold up against wind and storm
- Ah, it's the same for me.
- Is it over here or over there?
- Rather here!

Its blocking on computer and its need for coffee interrupts us. We meet behind the bar. A brief exchange on the London souvenir mug and the other mugs collected ended our conversation.

The mistake with the 4th Rome is the launch of the activity without having made available enough resources. Without having returned the copies they can't see their faults. But a house duty is necessary. This makes them work separately.

The session with the Venissia Pretoria Group is the first to have successfully built the vaults of all the teams. Often there is only one group that succeeds.

It is thanks to the passage and the recall on the technique with each team. The presence of positive elements in each of the teams also played a role.

Thursday January 30, 2020

The day seems to start well. Passing the reception, I meet in the corridor my old students, Célia, Claudia, Evanka and Lisa. They say hello in chorus.

In the session with 5th Vienna, I check the binders every time the students are on the computers. This is the favorite time for. The feeling of penalty for them is also a stimulus to get better organized next time.

The 4 Lisbon's are as talkative as usual. They are less pleasant. There is a little acceptance of comments on gossip. I put a very average rating on Victorines' transcript. I'm waiting for her reaction next time. The calm and the deep voice allow, to control, the movement of the session, without going to put negative points on the copies. But I put them on the list. It's the same procedure as the 4th Rome.

I go into the teachers' room. I find three arrogant people. Patrice, Marie Dax and

Elisa. I'm not saying hello. For once I do not feel embarrassed in such a situation.

I chat with Fabien. He talks about his life as a couple which stresses him and his ambition to cross America on a motorcycle. Obryan F gets in. We shake hands. I do not smile. I go back to the screen to ignore him right away.

Girls pass by on the reserve. It's Victoire, Charline, Galiane and a little sister of a certain Samira and other Nasrine.
We exchange a few words. I explain that the reserve is a common place for teachers. It's inaccessible to students. This is not the case for the class. They come up with a few words. Obryan B who leaves his class room, does not fail to slip from afar almost discreetly, "you are in recreation".
- Charline looks sad to me.
-        "No", answers Charline smiling.
- There you reassure me.
- "It's Samia. She is a nice one" Add Victoire.
- Am I supposed to know her?
- No, she replies.
- I wonder if she wouldn't be the little sister of someone I know!

- Nasrine. It's my sister.
- Nasrine goes to level "first" and Samira took the baccalaureate last year.
- Ah sir you have a good memory
- "I take time to know the names. But once known I do not forget them".

- But we, you knew us quickly.

- You? Yes, I know you from the start. But you are different.
The girls are quick to take leave.
- I'm not holding you back any more.
-       Good bye, sir.
-       Goodbye.
I meet Sicilia and Florine in the corridor.
- Hello sir in chorus and smile.
-       Hello.

It is 3:35 p.m. I continue to tinker in the reserve. I don't watch the 3rd Madrid going by. No sign. This ensures tranquility. Be forgotten. It becomes necessary to resume painting. No portrait in view, but painting is necessary.

Friday January 31, 2010

I collect the 6th Oslo. The session takes place in the most normal way in the world. I notice that Lynda has become a friend with Vitoria, and wants to immediately take her place from Lou to put herself on the right of Victoire. No one seems to want to discuss their wishes. I intervene and I urge Lou to stay in her place. Like the others. Lynda steps into the empty place. Before they go to computer, Lynda asks Victoire to put an object in her hands, in a military tone. Who does it belong to? In any case Victoire does not wait a second to execute.

I claim late homework. Both are at Lynda. She hands me her copy from her chair without even turning around. I see it and I ignore it. She then stands up and gives the sheet.

I perceive the disappointment of Victoire because of her rather average grade. I suggest to her at the end that she redo the work to increase her grade. In the name of the trust she had placed in me. When the bell rings, Lynda stops and looks at me. It's like waiting for a word from me about the last time. I cool her with a "Goodbye" in a neutral voice with a sweeping look. Then she leaves.

I had never found the 6th Oslo so less participative. They are not intuitive, nor cultivated. I then choose not to wait too long for the response each time. I display and let copy the answers. It is effective in saving time and much more restful for the nerves.

The 6th Brussels session is more enjoyable, efficient and full of participation. Positives waves are Giordan's idea. It is in full swing. When a positive mood is released, students produce endorphins that allow them to learn. Pauline is often amused and smiling.

The 4th Rome people are as talkative as usual. But deleting the words on paper prevents unlocking. I end up putting negatives on Naomys' copy.
- Yet it's her birthday?
- I answer "it's good, chance would have it".

It's the midday bell.
- Naomi, I need to talk to you
- No, I don't want to listen.
- How is it? Why?

- You put me on "negative points" while everyone is chatting.
- First it's not everyone, and then I've put others at least. Some people even reproach me for making you favoritism.

She smiles. She seems comforted.

She ends up promising to deserve the removal of the negatives. She is pleasant when leaving. I promise to remove the negatives if she deserves them next time.

I put a positive note to Roxane. Kahina on the other hand, I find her disheartened this time.

I conclude that we have to go back to basics. Entry into the classroom must begin with the row in the hallway and by waiting for standing silence, even if it means wasting time. The airlock to do the learner posture described by Patrice Meirieu is necessary.

A new class plan displayed on the board is required.

Samia is doing homework, maybe Spanish or English, while the technology homework is waiting to be done on her table. I recover it, tear it up and throw it in the trash. She doesn't cry but almost.

I do the same for Anna who drew. I keep calm throughout the session. The deep voice allows it but material preparation too.

With the 5th Prague, Florine discovers a new friend, Sicilia. Florine asks to sit next to Sicilia, in place of Ambrine, absent.

The students are pleasant and generally calm. Quasi-permanent observation and questions are the main control tools. There is Tuesday's mood that continues.

With the Pretoria, the session is as pleasant as the previous one. I make a mistake 10 minutes before the end. The video questionnaire is finished. I send the students to the computers. I should have kept the students in their place for paper work and accepted their disappointment. The same thing happened with the Prague instead. It is to be avoided.

The sixth ones, on the other hand, were able to start work on computer at 10 min before the ringing. This should be done again if necessary, as this is a start, in order to install the method.

I do not return the copies before the video. So a disturbance is avoided.

I meet Juliette in the hall, I am going for the 5th Tirana. She looks and then continues without saying anything. How to explain it? She is always in a bad mood? A lack of reflex, she is influenced by the blonde ponytail adder. There is perhaps some indifference due to absence? I have the choice of interpretation.

I arrive with the 5th Tirana in the hall. Marie Cecile greets me from afar then from close up, smiling. Janna also greets me in the parking lot from afar.

- Hello sir
- Goodbye Janna.

Madison, Leonie and Danna greet me all at once, laughing and smiling. They hadn't done it at the start of the New Year. It was the first for Madison since the start of the school year in September.

The session with the 5 Tirana begins and goes well. It's modeling on CATIAV5. But since I don't specify the purpose of the session, I change my objective during the session. At 15 minutes before the end they finish the test modeling, and some people shut down the computers without permission. Others are starting to walk around. They justify it's to help their comrades. You have to define the whole process, from the start the next time.

Saturday February 1, 2020

In town, I see Tiago, Clarisse and Juliette. They cross the street towards the post office. Clarisse turns around and smiles.

I see Victorine C twice in the shopping center. We don't even look at each other. Ambrine D recognizes me from afar, and greets me in passing.

Monday February 3, 2020.
I ask Lana to bring me the copies from a cupboard in the room where she has lessons with Obryan. A moment later I send Zoéline to pick up the bike. This is my way of creating contact between the two classes. It will facilitate the manufacturing sessions afterwards.

Lana must be happy to see her sister again. She had apostrophized her for a little while.

Janna is particularly discreet. They bring the table, she and Clementine, closer to the desk.

I start the sequence on braking. I give the document. I'm coming back to the office.

- Clementine! You have to make me think of Alezia.
- How was she? Asks Janna,
- She was flawless, serious. The perfect girl
- Are you in love with her? Replies Janna
- No, I'm not allowed to. I only knew her in sixth grade.
- Who did she get in 5th grade, Mrs. Mormon?
- No, Mr. Bonaparte.

It's a rather cold reaction. They did not know him, however.

- Is it possible to have you next year, as Florine?
- It's to be expected.
- How is she in class?
- She works in class. She likes practical activities.
- She has you in 6th, in 5th, she is lucky to have you.
- I don't know if she's happy to have me.
- Yes, she adores you.

I refrain from saying "it's reciprocal".

At the 3 p.m. break, Janna and Florine arrive. Janna claims her bottle. I let her pick it up in the other room. Then fill it in 112.
- I haven't done the card yet, warns Florine.
- I show a document, materials. This one is for Friday.

Thereafter I realize that it is the flowchart. It's a job she has to do again.

I talk to them without looking at them too often. I keep putting away the documents.
I have Florine right after. She is not very happy. Maybe the absence of some friend, Sicilia!

Tuesday February 04, 2020

From the start, some students who arrived first want to wait for the others to start. Exchange words with latecomers. I break this atmosphere immediately. I start the session and the fires revised downward. These are the 6th Tokyo.

Calypso keeps interrupting the explanations. I then decide to send her to the back of the class room. She was upset the whole session. Fantine requests that I write her a note.

When I leave the room, I hear no goodbye. And I say,

- Calypso still hasn't written a word of apology to me.
- Why writing, she could tell you. Replies Jacinte.

Tokyo returns at 11:15 a.m.
- Calypso!
-         Nothing. She answers and leaves.
- You have to write him a note. Because she is offended, claims Fantine.
- I too am upset.
-         She is sad.
- Ok, I promise to write her a word.

At noon I run into them in the corridor to give documents to others. They ask me again for writing. I promise to do it. They say goodbye to me several times. Fantine is very smiling. Calypso ends up smiling too. I resolve to write the word, to force him courteously to return the paper to me, I will ask in writing to respond in writing on the same paper after placing her at the back of the room for individual reading.

During the session of 6 Kiev, Juliette get in the class with a comrade. Request a foldable box. I do not know what it is. I'm going to reserve, I'm looking, I'm suggesting, it's not the right one I'm asking for Obryan's advice. They tell him it's the same as what he gave them the last time. Then I pass me a sheet of thin white plasticized paper. I give it to Juliette.

-       Thank you

-       Goodbye

I then find an interest in the regular inventory. In order to take note of the material available, there are so many. But I know I know more than anyone about the contents of the reserve because of so much storage and lots of use.

Thursday 05 February 2020

Victorine is absent. 4 Lisbon is calm. They even look a little sad. I refrain from asking them the reason. This way I avoid arousing them more than necessary. I realize that Victorine is the soul of this class.

Venissia always accompanies the second group of the 5 Pretoria. She is happy to work. This time I'm not making the previous mistake. I explain the purpose of the session and the sequence. So, none would say « I have finish ».

I go up the stairs, Madison runs along the corridor and she retraces her steps to say "Hello".

February 06, 2020

With the 5 Vienne, whose, Lisa and her Nasrine, the session is much more effective. The presentation of the objectives of the start sequence is well done.

The projection on the board in time of similar work on a computer enabled the explanation of geometric and graphic principles. The regular passage with the stick to show the functions on screen allows us to go faster.

With the 4 Lisbon, the session is much more pleasant than yesterday. Victorine is there. And she's happy to work well and get good grades. She has the gift of setting up a joyful and exciting climate, even if I sometimes have to reframe her gently. She said nothing about her rather average participation score. One of the five boys is guilty of turning off one of their two computers. I suspect Liam, I say nothing to her, but I ask the five to return to their places. For the not guilty I justify by their absence of surveillance. They never take things wrong. Some are seriously starting to work on paper.

I'm going to the yard. The weather is nice. I take a coffee and watch the class of old Kiev run. Madison is happy to see me and see me again with each pass. Her salvation and her radiant smile mean it every time.

It is 3:35 pm. I am working on the steering parallelogram in the reserve. I am standing in front of the work plan. The 3rd Madrid class park in front of the technology room waiting for their teacher. I don't watch them. I hear a girl call "Juliette". I see Lana passing for a moment. Towards the end I hear "Oh sir!" She waves with her hand, very smiling and delighted. She is very elegant with its light brown coat.
- Hello Juliette.

She continues, and a former comrade, Dubois, teases her with a word. She answers him with a little slap. She replies with a tap, and I throw.
-        Careful boy!

He turns around then returns and get in the classroom. He is the last one.

Madame wants to make us boring teachers. Teaching is an engineering profession. We create our own work. We don't execute.

Friday February 7, 2020

Rome arrives at 11:15 a.m. I let them get out of order. Some still standing, others already seated. All already returned. I then ask for a wave of the hand. There is silence. I'm thinking. Am I going to say the usual "hello sit down" so that they dive back into the almost usual din?
No. I'm going for it.
- When you come back, don't come and ask me anything at once. Neither go out nor change places, nor for anything else. From now on, I will always say no. When you do that, the session always starts badly and late. Wait for the session to start. That the instructions be given for the whole. Let the activity begin then I have time to deal with individual cases.

The potential voltage drops. There is calm. I invite them to sit down. The session is rather pleasant, even if I do not hesitate to notify negative copies of some students.

With the 5 Prague I do not make any formal gestures. I should have. It's a mistake. The session is unpleasant. I don't fail to tell them.

I'm asking for a Camilia G's notebook. She doesn't have it. I exclude her from class. Something I had never done in the establishment before. But we must mark the occasion. The session is quieter after that. She returns accompanied by Obryan the educational senior advisor. They arrive along the corridor. I anticipate and I go out so that they do not return. We have an exchange far from the classroom. I bring her in and Obryan tells her that she must have a remark on Monday. Camilia is not the meanest. She never fails to say hello in the hallway and outside. But she chats too much. When they leave the room, they all say goodbye. The students are very friendly outside the classroom.

The 5 Pretoria Class shows up at the door. I don't rush to bring them in. I ask them to wait. I close the door. I put the room in order and open the door for them.

Some people chat a little too much. Madame D walks down the hall to go to the furniture store. A moment later, she is accompanied by the head of the school. I need to find a way to reduce the hubbub to downpour, without raising my voice. I ask for silence then I demand the notebooks of Anna and Mattis, seated in two different places. I'm taking Loana away from Juliet. It brings calm.

But I still realize that I should have closed the door. It's more discreet for this kind of collective feedback session. I have to stay in the office to note the results, so it's more difficult to be calm.

At the break, Radia, Laure and Louise return. Radia asks what we are going to do in the next session. Louise is not concerned, but as she is there, I do not immediately dismiss the other two. I courteously explain the activity of the session. I even say at the end to Louise,

- If you want to come with the group one day, you can.

By going to get the 5 Tirana class, Charles Henri asked to be able to accompany the other group. I say yes in memory of the gift he made me at Christmas.

Louise arrives and asks the same thing. I answer yes for her as well as for Maéva and Eléna. I send Eliot away. He is very talkative.

During the session I discovered a less wise Louise. Chat when I explain, and have a little fun with the material. It's an error to place them together. Radia doesn't finish her work and turns off the computer.

Radia is always a bit like that, out of the frame, in opposite the lens. But in the future, it is understood that I will no longer accept the 5th ones to accompany the other group. The supervisor sent a paper asking why they were kept in the technology room. And their behavior deteriorates. It is better to leave technology to desire. Students can get tired of hearing and seeing the same activities.

I notice this bad habit that some people have when they have to help their comrade. They travel a little too much. They are not very focused on their own activity. They are not advancing. This creates an overly relaxed, less efficient and less serious atmosphere. This phenomenon caused an annoyance.

It is therefore necessary to prohibit anyone from moving from their computer to help another, without permission, on pain of being removed from the computer.

Lynda, in 6th Oslo, does her homework from the start of the session, when Victoire had not done so. The latter spends the clear of the session to finish it. Lynda participates quite seriously while Victoire is just having fun. I change her place for a moment so that she finishes her work. She finds herself with the very elegant Lou, far from their original place. Lynda takes her place and keeps Clara by her side.

With the 6 Brussels, the session is as pleasant as for the 6 Oslo. But Pauline commits odd things. I'm explaining to her, and for a moment she calls the assistant
- Gladys! The images, I can't order them.
- Thank you Pauline, I mean.

The assistant arrives and the other leaves. I resolve in the future to no longer value it by giving it the documents or materials to distribute.

I extend the activity on the computer to make sure that they all manage to do word processing with images from the Internet. Even if they don't all arrive at the same volume requested.

Monday February 10, 2020

It is 9 a.m. I'm going to see Damien to prepare Tuesday's gardening session. He describes me with disappointment in Elisa's choices, her lack of expertise and organization.
With the 6th Dublin and Tripoli, Clémentine and Janna bring their table closer to the office. Janna promises:
- Sir, we decided to be wise today
- I'm glad to hear it.

I ask to pick up the homework. Only two students did it, two boys, Victor and Jules. I then let the others do it in class.

The 5th Vienna session is enjoyable. Lisa saves participation every time. The session of the 5 Tirana reveals other students than Louise. I think it is necessary that I write to Louise to stimulate her.

The session of the 5 Tirana is always marked by moments of humor and sometimes of annoyance.

The session of the 5 Prague, in a group is very effective thanks to the separation of the students to work individually on computer.

The instructions are very clear. The projection is done. Explanations are made from time to time. I avoid showing annoyance. Except to say you have no reason to speak when I explain.

Sicilia, accompanied by Camilia, at the end of the session, asks,
- Sir, do you never make a positive remark.
- Yes, but I always thought that positive comments were made for those who rarely deserve it.
- They smile.

\- You often deserve it, and I tell myself when I should do it. But I promise you, I will find an opportunity for that.
-     Ok thank you goodbye
-     Goodbye

Tuesday February 11, 2020

The Tokyo session is very calm. Calypso is not very wise. I finally decide to separate Fantine from her friends. I'm setting up Fantine near Anna. I show patience, even when some are dragging on to complete a task.

I practically adopt the posture in 6 Kiev. But, the link is different. I only have links with Sophia, and in a limited way to the strict content of the course.
At 11:15 am Clarisse and Lana pass by, and return to the room. We chat for a while.
At 12:10 p.m. Alia returns with her glasses. She leaves them for me to fix them. She comes back to pick them up at 1:30 p.m. in room 113. I'm already with the Prague. She tries them, accompanied by Malya.
- They are well delivered.
- Great

- Thank you sir. Goodbye
- Goodbye.

With the Prague Gardening, the session begins calmly. Some students start chatting, but I keep calm. I sometimes ask for silence. I get it in a relative but acceptable way.

I repeatedly insist that they come out with something to write down and draw, then calculate.

I keep them busy so I can phone Damien to make sure he's coming. I am reassured.

Damien comes home. I ask him to explain the procedures. I don't find it captivating. I choose the secretaries with great difficulty.

When I ask them to get up to go out, I have to repeat several times for them to run. I do not understand the reason for their immobility. I keep patience.

We end up going out in the corridor. I hear them caught by Elisa, dissatisfied with the current plan.

- It's not like that. I prefer to do things in order. We need to get organized, she said to the students.

- Yes, but not in the hallway. We go there and organize things. I replied.

I go ahead and the students follow. Elisa goes too.

We end up managing three things fairly cordially. I finally convince to place two bins. We finish them. The students are happy to get involved.

I make every effort to courteously remove the task from Elisa's hands and place it in the hands of the students. Damien often agrees with me.

I spend the session involving the students in the activity. Some are withdrawn. If I gave free rein, Elisa would do everything alone and the students would be spectators. But Elisa always has the courtesy of not contradicting me, by facilitating real teamwork. I then stay the second hour with them to finish the seed of the two bins. I go back a few minutes in the room to put positive remarks to Sicilia and Camilia, allowing me to take the notebooks from their bags.

Elisa reminds the students.
- I still don't hear "goodbye Mister Yohan and thank you"
-        Good bye, sir
- Goodbye children.
   I had never found Sicilia so amiable before.

Wednesday, February 12, 2020

I get a 4 Rome rather properly tidy. When they return, a class plan is displayed. They take time to place themselves. A chat continues. I then ask everyone to stand up. There is silence.
- Hello. Sit down.
- Hello.

I explain the purpose of the session. I'm wrong not to get into the content of the session, focusing instead on catching up on homework. I then see a blatant lack of efficiency in most. I am nevertheless advancing a few who want to catch up on points in previous homework, to compensate for catastrophic marks.

Next time I start a session as a new activity, even if the activity is already covered. The specifics must be managed during the session and not as an objective, to allow everyone to launch on the same subject.

The great satisfaction of the session is the general mood. It's very pleasant. The rhetoric is worked on form and content. But that didn't stop the gossip. As usual, I request that requests be made in writing. Naomi makes an effort in the choice of paper, color, writing and style. Alia does less than the minimum service. No verb in the sentence. It's a successful session, though. No tension. Many have caught up on homework. It's consolidation.

The 5th Pretoria session is more effective. Firstly because I have the reflex to present the Smartphone supports already made, in order to stimulate and give meaning to the activity. Everyone works alone. At first it cools them. They end up finding the situation pleasant. I prevent class trips except to measure. Loana makes me think by her mistake at one point. When I explain a front view of an object, they look at it from my point of view and not from theirs. It is therefore necessary in the future to pose and explain an object, from a point of view common to all. At the end Loana says, it's nice to build things. Venissia had come the previous session with the other group. She is way ahead of the others. Not always a happy mood. But she does not seem to be bored in this matter.

It is 11:15 a.m. The 5th Santiago class, wait in the corridor for their technology teacher in front of the 115 room. I go to school life. I ask Elisa. She confirms that they do have Obryan B. He's busy with the phone ... she doesn't elaborate further. Thank you.... she continues. I arrive on the 1st floor I find Ingrid asking for silence. I say bring them in. Some are jostling and overthrowing Marius, already in bad shape, because of his prosthetics. I raise him immediately to prevent others from crushing him. I accompany him in his place. He is crying. Laurence, present, accompanies her to the infirmary. I make the call. I take pleasure in finding the old names. I then ask to go out and open the filing cabinets. I ask Juliette for her binder. I look, and find a workbook that has content. Well organized. Well structured, quite unlike those of my students. The main thing is to know what is being done as an activity. Obryan arrives around 11:30 a.m.

Thursday February 13, 2020.

The 5 Vienna class sessions' is going well. I repeat the introductory experience first with the models printed in previous years. That poses the situation. They are immediately interested. The projection facilitates the explanation in good time. But I no longer make the mistake of doing the session on the screen. I do tours. I give keys and tabs to click. It's much more effective. But this time I don't hesitate to take the student's smile to give a demonstration. What I avoided doing before. It goes faster. And the student sees and remembers easier. In general I solve the problem myself when it does not fall under strict instructions to follow.

The 4 Lisbon session is going as planned. I write a note to Victorine asking her to be "as exemplary as the last time". She takes it well, but she transmits the paper to the neighboring tables. I should have added a question with the word "answer:" so that she would have to give it back to me.

It is pleasant throughout the session. She tells me about her 12 which lowers the average. I then use it as blackmail so that it is applied throughout the session, under the promise that this note can be modified. She ends up rubbing off on Camilia to whom I launch "Camilia, work, do like Victorine". They help me put away the models. I involve them in wiring the model. Like the other comrades at his table, starting with Clara. She is excellence itself.

I'm innovating in relation to 4 Rome. I am not satisfied with specifying the beating portal document to use to reinvest knowledge. I take out the swing gate model, so that they can find similarities between the real components of the two models. It's 11:15 a.m., Sabia. C enters the reserve. I can't hear hello. I still say "hello madam". She does not answer. She looks and looks for something, without asking me anything, followed by Ingrid. Ingrid, she only salutes me.
- Hi. Ah, I have two at once. Ingrid goes on smiling.
Sabia turns around, smiles furtively and leaves.
In the hall, before noon, I see Elisa alone. So I'm going to take my coffee and chat with her.

- The students were interesting
-      Yes. But I prefer to be more organized. You need a plan
- How precisely?
-      Madam wants it done right. I would like the ground to be flattened, mowed.
- You are thinking long term. I wanted to finally start more concretely. Otherwise we would still wait for the return from vacation. And it's already dragging on.

-      Precise. How should things be done?

I ask several times to clarify what "doing things differently" means, and what planning. Elisa finds it very difficult to find the words to describe.
- Madame D said to me, "You are the pilot of the project". She wants there to be education beyond gardening, as meditation.
We then talked about Angelina, a new member of the group, still isolated. And Elisa offers Giovanni to be her friend.

The concern with Elisa is that she talks a lot about planning. But she doesn't plan anything, and does even less concrete things. However, she has the know-how. But she never comes to see me to ask me what we're going to do. I then find that Damien is much more responsive and available.

At 2:20 p.m., I meet Damien in the corridor. We talk about watering the tubs.
- Last week, she wanted to sow in pots and leave in the boiler room. I tell him it's no use. She doesn't want to hear anything. She thinks I can take care of it, water them
- She made them?
-         Yes. But saw you on Tuesday. Everything is gone. Everything is dead.
- Is there any way to level the ground?
- Yes, with a spade and a rake. I show how to do it. Then I give the materials.
-         Here is. So she wants everything to be done, but she does nothing.

It is 3:43 pm, the 3rd Madrid pass in the corridor, preceded by their technology teacher. In the middle, Juliette turns, smiling, waving at her.
-         Hello sir.
- Hello Juliette.
A comrade Fernandine, and a comrade Charles, almost try to dissuade her from it. She was so embarrassing for those who came

behind her. They are followed by Marie Dax in conversation with Lana.

Juliette alone does the week. How to keep from drawing it again?

Friday February 14, 2020.

It is 8:15 a.m. I'm going to get my 6th. I pass in the rank of the 5 Santiago. I'm looking for Juliette the brown. It comes from far away. His comrades call him. Her friends follow her, and I wave.
- If possible that I see Juliette in private.
- Hello Juliet
- Hello sir
- can you do me a favor?
- Yes
- Marius, is he there?
- Normally yes. She glances around.
- do you talk to him sometimes?
- Yes of course.
- I would like you to see him later. You say "hello, how are you?" "
- For his prosthesis?
-Yes, for all his trouble.
-OK no problem.

- It's very nice thank you.
The Oslo session doesn't really impress. Especially since the participation is not very lively.
I am however beginning to have a crush on the 6 Brussels. Especially since the "School assistant" are absent today. They become warm. Pauline is always very cheerful. It's the charm of class.
At 10:10 am, Juliette returned to the classroom.
- Juliet...!
- I saw Marius, he said he was fine.
- It's nice of you. When his comrades come to hear from him, he feels less alone. The primary goal is that he feels less of the burden of the disease. Right now he's doing chemo. He is in bad shape. There he will be happy to feel supported.

- Yes. Juliette's smile is radiant. I forgot how kind she was.
- It's very kind of you. Thank you. Goodbye.
- Good bye, sir.

The Rome session always has inertia and ineffectiveness. I request that all requests be made in writing. This greatly limits chat and downtime. I no longer respond individually at any time. I choose the moment to respond. It's much more effective.

I cool Agatha's mood at the end because she allowed during the session in Naomi to cheat on his duty. And she was revising Spanish instead to do the tech work. She also chats endlessly. I get his Spanish card.

I'm waiting. I'm procrastinating. For a moment I see her mimicking a dance, sitting still. I do not hold back, I tear the card and throw it in the trash. At the end she comes to claim it. I then unpack all the annoyance contained so far on their chatter and their notes obtained easily while they are often stressed for other subjects.

The session is rather calm, because I take the time to look at them and to question them. They go to the board one by one. They all fail to wire first. I'm making a point. Some are starting to find the right ways to do it.

Samia comes to see me for her work. I explain it her. She doesn't seem to want to hear. I give him another document. She makes even more mistakes. I say to him, "It is very badly done. You don't want to listen

to me. "I asked you to redo it in pencil on the draft, before copying it on a clean paper. You do it again on the clean and in pen! ".
- Look at Kahina. She listens to me and she remains positive.
- She's lying to you.
-      Yes maybe. But she lies with great courtesy.
- Kahina smiles.

Towards the end of the session, I see the results below the objectives. I remember the bad mood. I repress brittle thoughts for latecomers and cheaters. I show a completely optimistic face. The session is rather saved.

With the Prague, the session goes on as usual. A heavy and tense start and the atmosphere become pleasant as you go along.

I collect the notebooks of Marie, Camilia and Edene.

I require that all requests be made in writing. The three girls write nice words to me for Valentine's Day and the holidays. They thus manage to calm the mood. I return the notebooks at the end without notifying anything.

The next session with the Pretoria begins with some gossip, which is difficult to contain. I warn then, calmly.

- You'd better stop chatting. Otherwise the sessions will be boring. I will choose the facility. If some have requests, it can only be done in writing.

They calm down. Some dissatisfied with their places, write and put the paper in the box.

They get into writing quite easily. I explain the interest that is noticed right away. There is calm, useful communication and little complaints. It sounds the break time.
Louise comes in and asks to put down her bag, smiling. During the session she is ahead of her comrades in modeling on CATIAV5.

Monday March 2, 2020

Zoéline T shouts at Victor. No, this is my place. Don't take my place.
- Zoéline! Come here please. Can I ask you something?
- Yes,
- You're going to see Victor. You say "sorry", and "you can take my place"
- Why this?

- Firstly because you will no longer need it, and then ... and there I refrain from telling her "you are the most lovable"... I simply say to her "I would like you to do that for me, that would be nice".
-        Okay.

A moment later I find Victor in his place.
Jana and Lisa arrive before Nasrine. They want to sit together and kick Nasrine out of her place. Nasrine spends the session in a moody mood.
- Why is Nasrine sad?
- Because I'm fired from my place.
Lisa tells her again at the end of the session. "You are no longer in this place".
Nasrine and Jana both want to have Lisa.

Octavia brings me her copy. I point out her some errors. I think I'm doing her a favor. She corrects them. In the next assignment, she brings back her copy. Questions were not answered. I report them to him. She takes her copy and breaths all her exasperation. Louise observes, seems surprised and has fun. She gives me her copy. I point out some faults to him. She gently begins to rectify them.

I run to Octavia.
- I thought I was doing you a favor. But you find that I penalize you. Do you want to return your copy?
-       Yes

She brings back her copy. The session remains very pleasant. There is a good general spirit in the class. But I also showed calm and a sense of distribution.

The Prague session is the worst of the week. Florine shows a bad mood. The Edene group arrives late and chats on the way home. Respect is now the only important criterion. I will no longer let the students come in late. The first wave must return, start the session by letting the latecomers wait in silence, demanded in the corridor.

Florine said "goodbye" when she left, while Iris said nothing. Yet she had worked well, with a touch of smugness and a sly smile certainly, but satisfactory.

Tuesday 03 March 2020.
I crop the 6th Topazes several times calmly because of the comments. I send Calypso to the bottom. They end up listening.

Fantine is forced to make a presentation on braking. She refused. She does it great after all.

The 6th Kievs are very lively, active and happy. Sofia is very radiant. I thought I had cooled her down with the requirement of respect for the forms during his presentation. She keeps coming back and asking to go to the board again.

It is a class with which I had no real connection, neither collective nor individual. But there is beginning to be a return of positive waves.

Both sessions were successful, in substance and form. I present the techniques of a good oral from the start. At each stage we take stock and we start again. As they go along, they perfect the way. They acquire vocabulary, a method and technical reasoning.

They are not unhappy not to have touched the computers.

It is 2 p.m. I go into the teachers' room. There's only Elisa. She is copying a text from the pen from his Smartphone.

- What can we do next Tuesday?

- It all depends on the weather.
- What if the weather is nice?
-             I do not know. We may continue to….
- "You said the key word, the main idea. We have to continue.

   During her answers, she does not look up. She doesn't stop writing. Pierre gets in the room. We greet each other from afar. He is always smiling and fun.
- Maybe we'll go see the seeds later. She adds
- Maybe I'll come with you.
- Wouldn't you be jealous?
-             I am very jealous. If the students tell me "we like this teacher" I ask "what about me?" "
- It's funny stone. He laughs with me. But that doesn't make Elisa smile at all. She takes everything in the first degree.
- If you're jealous, we're not going to get along.
- I would only like to see at least the same time as the students. I prefer not to arrive in front of less knowing pupils.
- Pierre, amused, smiles.
She doesn't seem to be delighted that I am accompanying them. What I decide to cancel.

I'm going to the hall. I meet Damien and we discuss the work to do the next session.

Elisa goes out and doesn't miss a thing. The other supervisors are also watching.

I'm on the reserve. Marie and Camilia sent by Elisa to retrieve the agrarian calendars. She knew it was Damien who had them. I promise to call Damien to bring them back. Five minutes later he brings them back.

Evanka K and Lisa J come down the hall to say hello. They just had technology. They are cheerful, smiling and very kind. I do not keep them long. They were the old Prague. It is 2:25 p.m. I make the Prague wait while waiting for Elisa, who must arrive. She is in the hall, not knowing where the Prague class is. So I send Lyna to her.

Lisa greets me from a distance when I am not even looking at her.

Thursday 05 March 2020

4 Lisbon is like a great moment of positive influence. Victorine does not stop participating. She is enthusiastic. After 15 minutes she tends to get short of breath.

- Victorine, you lasted 15 minutes in an exemplary fashion. Try to keep up. Another 40 minutes. Be tough.
- Laughs from the whole table.

I question Victorine, who gives twice the wrong answer. I courteously forbid her friends from whispering the answer to her. Emma still seems to whisper "Micro switch" to her. She then responds with enthusiasm, happy to put herself forward. Her comrades applaud her. Then the whole class follows.
- Edgar! Before you clap, finish your work.
- Laugh at the class.

I would have done well to say that it was Emma who had breathed the word to him. I don't think so at all. Besides, Victorine, who found the answer for the sliding document gate, continues to identify this same component on the cylinder. This means that the Pygmalion effect keeps her in her persistence. It is worth putting its flaws on the lack of reflection time. But the energy and the positive radiance it gives off is half of what the whole class provides.
- Victorine, you want to help me put this portal away.

- Laugh at Camilia.
- I always demand the perfection of Victorine.
- The smile continues.
- Liam! Stay in touch with the right situation.
- Aylan, you changed places without telling me. Stay there. But I'm watching.
I raise Aylan twice to do his job. For a moment he has fun and makes his comrades laugh.
- Aylan, I warned you. You are going to change places.

Lally, I warned you and Barthélemy. Before my eyes instead of participating you chat. You have been warned. You will change places next time. I have reason to believe that the results will change. I think she understands there that she can no longer copy her homework, at least no longer compare it to that of Coline and Clara who always rhyme with rigor and perfection.

With the 5 Vienna, I first set out the objective and the approach as long as the students are receptive, in the early morning hours.

In the middle of the session I make a point of the lack of physical contact between them and the technical objects placed on the table. However, I had given orders to come and observe, hold and measure. It's technology. You cannot remain confined to the text or the drawing without ever approaching, touching and observing. You must have more curiosity. What does it look like? It's hard? It's soft? It's light? It is heavy? They seem to be aware of what they are hearing at this point.

Lisa has not finished. She tries to help Nasrine and Jana.

- Lisa, I prefer that you finish first. It will allow me to see what you understand.

She ends up finding pleasure in getting ahead and creating less usual shapes. She makes a void in the middle of the model in the form of an ellipse. It sounds and she absolutely wants to finish it before leaving. I give her one example and she does another. She's seems really happy with it.

I often think of what Patrice Meirieu recommends. Let the student help his classmate to learn more. But perhaps he will learn even more if he feels a positive offset from his surroundings by crossing the barriers. I adopt this approach in the desire to activate the levers of a differentiated teaching. So the students begin to learn, each at their own pace.

When I focus on the connection with object, I take care to note that some of the pupils, in this case, Lisa, Jana and Nasrine, are in line with the expectations outlined.

Monday March 9, 2020

It is 9:15 a.m. I pass in the corridor of the first. I see at the end a student, a certain Célina B. She is looking at me no doubt wishing that I intervene so that a supervisor comes to open the elevator for her. I don't do that. I look at her then I ignore her, in memory of his arrogance at the end of last year games. I give her advice and she replies "I know I know". And she hasn't said hello since. Finally she didn't know.

It is 10 a.m. A student I don't know comes to see me for the elevator. - There is nobody - I'm calling, there's no one
- I call I am told we will send someone

- There is still no one.
- I come down to school life,
- Elisa, there is a student who has been waiting for the elevator for a while
- I don't have the keys. It's Mr. Fernand.
I will then see Obryan F.
- Hello Obryan. Do you have the keys to the elevator? Kid has been waiting for a while.
- I don't have the keys. It's Fabien.
I am getting up. I find the boy in conversation with music colleague Carole.
- I haven't found anyone who has the keys.
I go back down after the end of the break, I find Fabien in the hall pushing a rant in front of a class which seems too talkative while going towards the permanence. I come from behind. I grab her by my left arm to get her attention.
- Do you have the keys of the elevator? I ask him discreetly.
-       Yes. He takes them out of his pocket, I think I have them. He holds them back by closing his hand. The class is watching. This is a 5th grade class that I know. It's maybe the 5th Tirana.
- There's a kid who's been waiting for the elevator for 20 minutes, always discreetly, but in a more serious tone.

\- I have already been there.
- No, not this one
- I did all the floors.
- We're going to go see. I ask.
- I went to see right now.
\- It's wrong. I retorted aloud, following him behind.

We stagnate a little at the crossroads near the reception. The exchange goes more and more tense. I signal to go back up.
- We're going to go back up, we ask the student.

It turns out that the student must have moved when the supervisor came.

We still continue the exchange, missing to come up with more manly and personal courtesies. We meet at the bottom, we continue, and there other supervisors were present.

The reality was that I didn't give a damn if he was telling the truth or not. All I wanted was scream louder than him. I want only to show that I'm not being yelled at. That's for sure.

I'm doing the 6 Dublin Tripoli, maintaining a certain level of standards. But that was only seen towards the end. The session begins with my claim for homework. The majority had not done so. I then let those concerned finish or make their own. And I send the others to the computers, to make a synthesis on Word of the manufacturing processes. It's as tempo activity, but very useful. It also penalizes latecomers.

Tuesday March 10, 2020

Someone knocks on the door. Madame D. opens the door, accompanied by the guardianship, Mr. Martens and another.
- Hello
- Hello,
- We just pass.
- You are welcome.
- I signal the students to get up without her seeing me.
- She beckons them to sit still without me seeing her.
- Goodbye
- Goodbye

It is 10:10 a.m. Florine and Gwendoline show up at the door.
- We come to ask you if we can register with the library.

- Today is not sunny. We are not going to do gardening. In addition we will have two delegates less. So you can go to the library.
- Florine hesitating. As if to wait until I express my disappointment at his absence. I hold myself back.
- Ok you can go to the library.
-         Thank You! Good bye.
- Goodbye. See you Friday.

With the Kievs, I have been ranting several times. Baris is the first on student who does not bother to finish the assignment or open the notebook on the right lesson, let alone use the square to draw a right angle. He has one, but he preferred to say that he did not. I spend time with him, but he ends up taking him out and finishing his work properly. I push some of them to get to the bottom of it. No, so that they retain knowledge but more so that they come out of defeatism and ease. They must read and look for concepts in the notebook. We cannot suggest that a Dys student is in difficulty in technology but comfortable in other less practical subjects where we touch less object. Candys H kept smiling until the end. Even with all the requirements of perfection that I imposed on them before to let they join their comrades.

I started the tempo activity of the students who are getting ahead, since a few days because of the latecomers in the homework. Sofia does a duty very poorly and half done. I encourage him to finish it. I want first by, flattering her ego by recalling the previous session.
- I did not understand this exercise
- This is the same exercise you did orally a week ago. You would have done the session alone if I had left you the choice.
- Sofia laughing.
She finishes her duty.

Few respect the instruction from most of them, not to go to "images" but to go to "All" and then to "Wikipedia". And this is where I have a prolonged blood stroke. But the mistake is that I didn't write it on the board. I would have avoided repeating it to everyone, by simply remembering to apply the instruction.

In reality I avoid writing the instructions, because they do not understand when I say note this and it is not necessary to note that. The memory is very short. They forget the oral instructions. So it's better to leave everything down, but abbreviate. And it's good that they keep a record in the notebook.

I then choose to make an oral assessment. I install a pleasant climate, followed by the distribution of the teams or I set up the discreet writing to communicate their wishes to me. I thus manage to make balanced choices even if some are not chosen by anyone, like Barthélemy and Clémentine. Sophia is the most requested. Like Fantine in 6 Tokyo.

Wednesday, March 11, 2020

The session of the 4 Rome takes place with more calm than usual and more participation, but in a cold atmosphere.

I start rather dry. I'm getting an assignment, and a lot of people hadn't done it. I give them time to do it or finish it. Unlike usual, I separate the copies well laggards from those of others. I warn them. The scale applies to it.

I see a student revising moral and civic education courses. They seem to have exam

afterwards. I collect his cards. I refrain from tearing them apart. And the perverse effect of this discreet patience is that many do the same. They revise in a less discreet way. I then confiscate the cards one after the other. Of which Naomi, who seems to be the most dissatisfied.
- I prefer that you put a remark in the notebook, she defends herself
- Precisely, it's because you prefer a remark in the notebook that I don't make any. You will not have the documents until tomorrow.
I go into the teachers' room. I find there, Jean Marc, a supervisor and Fabien.
- Hello gentlemen
-         Hello
I'm approaching the coffee maker.
- There is coffee, says Fabien.
- Ah, when Fabien is there, I have no fear. The coffee is hot too.
We then discuss the management of Wednesday deductions. Fabien is a blood without bitterness. Exactly like me.

Thursday March 12, 2020

I'll get the 5 Vienna. I meet Calypso, Jacinte and Fantine in the hall. They ostensibly ignore me. I had agreed to put

Fantine with her friends to make the Dragster, with the condition that they are wise.

I pass near the 5 Prague. They send a very warm hello in numbers. They don't seem unhappy with the last two or three sessions.

With the 5 Vienna, I see the virtues of a document well done in less than an hour. Whereas I had the annoying habit of launching activities without any written and diagrammed support apart from the material objects.

So in short, the best thing is that, at the start of a sequence, it is better to get out of the usual perfectionism. I was waiting to finish a document before offering it to the students. It is better to concoct an especially schematic deposit document, preferably A4, in there, putting the main information, especially the right title, even if it has a lot of imperfections.

The 4 Lisbon class returns and go to their old places. They probably count on my inattention. I'm waiting for everyone to get to their place. I'm posting the recent plan and asking everyone to stick to it.

I return the copies and many complaints start at the office preventing the session from starting. I therefore demand that any claim of any kind be made in writing.
Victorine disappointed with her bad. I wait a moment and suggest that she do the homework again. Igor wants to change the group. I wait a bit before motioning for her to go near Liam.

There is chatter at times, and I warn them.
- If you chat like that, the first consequence is that I do not have time to let you finish here the noted work, and you will have a lot of homework.

There is calm. It's no longer difficult to silence them after that. Just call one or two first names.

On the educational level, the session is successful thanks to better preparation. Preparation consists of looking at the document and thinking about the right questions to ask in order to connect them to the content, leading them to find a link between what they have seen and done, and the document. By giving a precise meaning to the vocabulary read. Based first on the physical model, with words they had seen previously and not with the new document. Because it happens that the same type of content falls flat, so the questions are too directly asked to fill in the gaps without further thought or reminder.

Other factors are behind the satisfaction of the pedagogical aspect. I'm not too lazy to go and find the right-file to show and recall the acquaintances. I often get up when I ask questions. I am in a certain physical dynamism, while avoiding speaking while walking.

Among the words of complaints, there is one "I love you, you are the best teacher" there is strong chance it came from Liam. As a student reads a text, I keep reading the words, and they understand when I get to that one. A burst of general laughter interrupts the reading for a moment.

In terms of atmosphere, it is no different from the previous ones. Some positivity radiates. They are nice. Even if warnings I have made several.

But I had to move around the room at times to be calm. I notice the difference there. We must not stop occupying the space to control it. I observe so I warn some gestures and dissuade it.

It is 2:25 p.m. I'm on the reserve. Three student of Georgetown class arrive in front of the technology room, opposite. They are waiting for the colleague. He is late to come. The pupils are less and less wise. Already, that class is the least wise of the 3rd level. It mainly consists of the 5 Jakarta from 2 years ago, and the 4 Rome from last year. The latter is truly the last on the whole line.
I go out into the corridor.
- The 3rd! Line up.

The supervisor arrived as reinforcements in the corridor. I'm going get a big boy, who intrudes into the permanence room. I grab him by the arm. I almost kick him.
I bring them in. Embarrassing ways and behaviors begin to say the least. They are standing. I make discreet and individual gestures to dissuade certain deviations in behavior. It works. I wait for the silence before inviting them to sit.

- Hello! Sit down
- Hello sir.
- Take out your technology binder. Open it on the right page.
Some have to finish the presentation on the wind turbine. I therefore insist that some people finish the text in question without hiding my knowledge of the subject.

I choose the conciliatory attitude. I avoid the severity that generates laughter and sanctions. The session is lined with annoyance and breathtaking tension.

I crop courteously. I ask two students for notebooks. I change places to others to finish a job. I authorize two serious students to go to computer to finish a physics work.
The session is rather chatty but in an acceptable level of sound and general behavior.

Friday March 13, 2020.
It's the last day before confinement.

Sicilia asks to go on computers to do 3D modeling. I don't have a choice. It is a mistake. I should have made them practice.

They are even easier to master. Besides, especially for these fifth year classes, where many do not do homework, or finish it, computerization is a lever to focus on individualities. Provided they get document which guarantees autonomy. It's made available. Classroom practice is a culmination of pedagogy. It's learning by doing. It is the transformation of learned knowledge into know-how. We must therefore be attentive to student complaints. Time to step back and reflect is always necessary to know the relevance of the students' complaints.